Igniting the Leader Within

The Leadership Legacy of Ben Franklin,
Father of the American Fire Service

Igniting the Leader Within

The Leadership Legacy of Ben Franklin,
Father of the American Fire Service

BY MICHAEL F. STALEY

FIRE ENGINEERING®

PennWell
MEDIA FOR STRATEGIC MARKETS   SINCE 1910

Copyright © 1998 by Fire Engineering Books & Videos, a Division of PennWell Publishing Company

Published by Fire Engineering Books & Videos
A Division of PennWell Publishing Company
Park 80 West, Plaza 2
Saddle Brook, NJ 07663
United States of America

Book Design: Max Design
Cover Design: David Derr

Printed in the United States of America

10 9 8 7 6 5 4 3 2 1

Library of Congress Cataloging-in-Publication Data

Staley, Michael F., 1955-
  Igniting the leader within : the leadership legacy of Ben Franklin, father of the American fire service / by Michael F. Staley.
    p.   cm.
  ISBN 0-912212-71-3 (softcover)
  1. Fire extinction—Vocational guidance.   2. Fire departments—
Management. 3. Leadership. 4. Fire fighters—Job satisfaction.
I. Title.
TH9119.S73   1998
363.37'023--dc21   98-36742
                                                                      CIP

Dedication

This book is dedicated to both of my families. Like all firefighters, I have two. First, there's my "real" family; and second, there are the brothers and sisters of fire and rescue with whom I have been proud to serve and share my life. This book is for all of you.

Acknowledgments

I *gniting the Leader Within* has been a joy to write, but I didn't do it alone. I have a lot of people to thank. First, I thank my loving wife Kate, who patiently tolerated long hours of work and travel away from home. I thank my mother, Jo, that Army nurse who reared me alone. I thank my father, Victor, who never saw my life develop but who has watched over me in the many years he's been gone. I thank Bev Browning, my researcher and friend. I gratefully acknowledge Bill Manning, Diane Feldman, Brian Hendrickson, and Rob Maloney of *Fire Engineering* magazine for their guidance and vision. I thank Jim Morneweck, who gave me my start as a firefighter when he first asked me to join West Mead District One. I thank my mentor and friend Jim Bell, who allowed me at age 16 to be the youngest member of the Crawford County Firemen's Association. I thank Chief George Hamburger and the men and women of the Erie Fire Department who told me that I had enough moxie to become a career firefighter. I thank the men and women of the Volusia County (FL) Emergency Medical Services, who welcomed me in 1973, helped me develop my skills, and saved my life in 1990. I gratefully acknowledge the men and women from the City of Port Orange (FL) Department of Fire and Rescue, who helped me make a positive difference every day and who taught me much of what I know about leadership. I particularly thank the E-172 crew: DE Richard Tufano, PM Tom Bazanos, FF Jim Whitmarsh, and FF Joe DiBella, the brother who mowed my yard for a year after my accident and never accepted more than a drink of water. I thank Norman Lewis, who gave me the opportunity to join the faculty of the Daytona Beach Community College and helped me realize that I would learn so much when I taught. I gratefully acknowledge the faculty, staff, and students of the National Fire Academy who share my enthusiasm for our profession by advancing life safety and fire prevention programs that are used throughout the world. Finally, I thank the many friends in the fire and rescue service who have given me the benefit of their ideas, experience, and support for *Igniting the Leader Within*. This work belongs to all of us.

About the Author

Michael F. Staley is a motivational speaker and head of Golden Hour Motivational Resources of Port Orange, Florida. A veteran firefighter and EMT, he has served with the West Mead District 1 Volunteer Fire Department of Meadeville, Pennsylvania; the Volusia County (FL) Emergency Medical Services; and the Port Orange (FL) Department of Fire Rescue. In 1990, he was critically injured in an accident involving two cars at the Daytona International Speedway. He made a miraculous recovery and now travels around the United States and Canada delivering a message of hope, encouragement, and motivation to various organizations.

Table of Contents

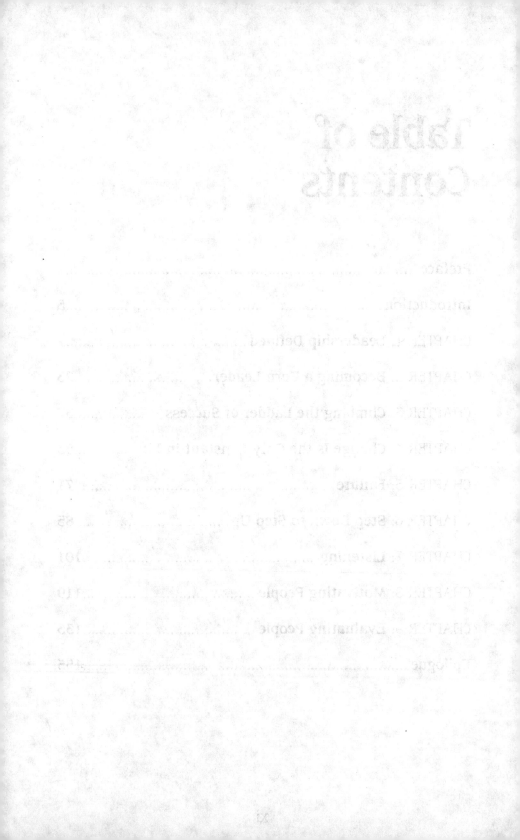

Preface

On February 11, 1990, I was working as a firefighter-paramedic at Daytona International Speedway. It had been a day of accidents. My partner Ken Elliott and I were stationed in our ambulance, keeping an alert eye on Calamity Corner, a dangerous turn on the track notorious for throwing cars and drivers into chaos.

With only five laps to go in a 200-mile race, we heard that familiar, sickening sound of impact and turned around to see Car 58 limping into the infield. The driver didn't appear to be moving. We were dispatched immediately and pulled up behind the crippled car. Leaping out, I sprinted to the driver's window and leaned in to check him out. Accident procedures are very clear for everyone at the Speedway when an accident takes place. I didn't even have to look up to know that my partner was poised for action, waiting for my signal to respond. From years of experience, I knew that the other cars were still on the track, anxiously lining up under the direction of the caution flag. Everything should have been by the book, but something was about to go terribly wrong.

The drivers behind the caution flag were jockeying, unwilling to lose their hard-won positions and eager to take advantage of the faster drivers' mandate to slow down. They crowded each other. As the pack lapped Calamity Corner again, someone bumped Car 29, sending it out of control. It came screaming off the track, rocketing across the infield and slamming into Car 58, broadsiding the passenger door at 160 mph. I saw it coming, but there was nothing I could do. The impact hurled me out of the driver's window and into the air. I came down in the path of Car 29, which was now traveling sideways, and I was trapped under 3,500 pounds of race car. Worse, I was wedged under the searing exhaust manifold.

My partner and other medical professionals on duty at the Speedway were there instantly. As they struggled to pull me out from under the car, they began what I now refer to as the "Roll Call of Love." One after the other called to me: "It's me, Mike. I'm here for you, buddy." I couldn't answer because the weight of the car was crushing my chest. As my friends pulled me out from under the car, stabilized me, and established an airway so I could breathe on my own again, I looked into my partner Ken Elliott's eyes and took his hand. Both of us felt an electric connection that spoke louder than words. I could hear the chop-chop-chop of helicopter blades and felt the wind in my face. I thought to myself, "Oh, no. Good news doesn't travel by chopper." I was right.

I was evacuated to Halifax Hospital Trauma Center in Daytona Beach, where I had brought so many patients of my own in the past. The staff knew me well, but on that day no one recognized me. When my friends on the trauma team realized that it was one of their own on the table—and I was in bad shape—there were tears. One nurse, with whose family I had eaten supper the week before, was so badly shaken that she had to be relieved of duty. I was diagnosed as having lacerations; puncture wounds; avulsions; first-, second-, and third-degree burns; fractures of both legs and knees; a concussion; severe internal bruising; and 100 fractures in my left arm.

I struggled against the pain and fear as the trauma team worked. I was doing a good job of holding my emotions in check until the orthopedic surgeon leaned over and told me that he was going to have to amputate my left arm. For the first time since the ordeal began, I cried. Speaking was difficult, but I whispered, "Good news: won sailboat race. Bad news: left-handed." The confused surgeon turned to the trauma team for interpretation. It was easy for those who knew me—I am an accomplished sailor. The weekend before, I had beaten three out of five of the best catamaran sailors in the United States. Losing my left arm was out of the question as long as there were two more left to defeat, let alone a life to live. The surgeon instantly decided to fight to save my arm. Using bone grafts from my hips, he rebuilt my arm with 14 inches of metal plate and 26 screws. One hundred people volunteered to give blood. The healing began.

I like to think I took charge from the beginning. On my mom's first trip to my bedside, I tried to soothe her by speaking of my great faith. "Jo, this didn't happen to me. It happened for others. There's a reason. Let's just wait and see what it is."

I told my physical therapist that it was my intention to give 110 percent effort every day and that I expected the same from the physical therapy team. The physical therapist obviously was alarmed at this burst of overenthusiasm, so I compassionately added, "But I know that you're going to have bad days from time to time. On those days, you can give 107 percent." Laughingly, he agreed.

My comeback trail was arduous and miraculous. Starting with such monumental tasks as rolling over in bed assisted by three people and graduating to Herculean efforts like tying my shoe (this took more than a year to master), I battled my way through 8,600 hours of therapy. Over my bed in the nursing home hung a medal engraved with the words "Best Flip. Worst Landing." My friends started calling me Lucky.

But "lucky" is an elusive quality, like shadows and sunlight on a narrow path. Through months of hard work, I struggled back to health; however, I was unable to rehabilitate sufficiently or quickly enough to pass the annual physical proficiency tests required of all firefighters, and I lost my position with the Port Orange Department of Fire Rescue. Who could blame them? They needed able-bodied firefighters who could save lives, and I was still struggling to tie my shoe. I went from being the most decorated firefighter in Florida to being unemployed. My life had changed forever.

As in all major transformations, something's lost and something's gained. I lost my career, but I gained the valuable insights into life and love that only come from a brush with death. I took the "Golden Hour"—that critical time following an injury during which a trauma team has the greatest chance of saving a life—and turned it into a life-affirming mission and the name of my company, Golden Hour Motivational Resources. I took my new nickname, Lucky, and designed a four-leaf clover logo that has become my trademark. Each leaf reflects a philosophy I developed during my transformation:

1. Life is too long if you don't enjoy every breath of it.
2. Commitment is loyalty to oneself.

3. We use the attitude we choose.
4. Choice, not chance, determines destiny.

My first forays onto the stage with my lucky four-leaf clover were to say, "Thank you for your support!" I wanted to get up in public to express my appreciation and let my friends and neighbors see that I was all right and continuing with my lifelong mission to make a positive difference in the world every day. Only now, I would be trading in the big red truck of fire rescue for a microphone. I started with fire rescue colleagues, rehabilitation professionals, schoolchildren, civic organizations, and medical staffs, all of whom had stood by me with love and concern during my recovery. My audiences understood very clearly what I was trying to say, because it didn't take long before I was getting calls for speaking engagements all over the country.

Today, as a successful motivational speaker and teacher, I take the lessons I have learned and the truths I know and offer them to enthusiastic audiences from one end of the continent to the other. My lucky four-leaf clover has been carried by members of the White House Secret Service staff and firefighters in the remote regions of Manitoba, Canada. It has accompanied rescue workers in the Oklahoma City Bombing and been taped to the notebook covers of schoolchildren in Florida. From the courtroom to the boardroom, from the locker room to the schoolroom, I have carried my messages of success. Transformed from a decorated fire rescue officer to an Arsonist of the Mind, I now devote my life to igniting the inner being of others.

Introduction

There's a disquieting shift taking place in your career. You feel it coming, heralded by the distant rumble of thunder that signals a storm brewing before you can even see it. Like an unseen storm, it's dangerous ... and exciting. There's nothing you can do to stop it. You can only scramble to prepare for it, hoping you'll know when to meet it head-on to harness its energy and when to duck for cover to keep from getting struck by lightning. Change is on the horizon. It's time to step up and claim your place as a leader.

Storm Warnings

You've recognized the signs that you are no longer satisfied with your job. You sneaked into the chief's office when no one was around and sat in the big chair just to try it on for size ... and discovered that you like the fit. You received yet another report from "The Top" and secretly concluded with some certainty that "I could have done this better." You found yourself suddenly embarrassed by your badge because your rank is too low, your title is too modest, and you're missing important initials after your name.

So you signed up for the company in-service training programs, went to the library and checked out all the books on management, and bought all the audiotapes. You're making subtle changes in your appearance, taking an extra few minutes to polish your shoes and press your slacks before coming to work. You've tightened up your work habits, coming in a little earlier and leaving a little later than you used to. You are working out a strategy for deflecting all of the disparaging remarks from your fellow firefighters who grumble about your "brownnosing" and "sucking up" to management. You are quieting the suspicions of management, who can't quite comprehend your sudden interest in them. You're doing it all because you finally know what you want.

You want a promotion.

And nothing will ever be quite the same.

Let's get started.

CHAPTER 1

Leadership Defined

"We learn by chess the habit of not being discouraged by present bad appearance in the state of our affairs, the habit of hoping for a favorable change, and that of persevering in the search of resource."
—Ben Franklin

So, once you've made the decision to put your career on the promotion track and head for the top, how do you get the skills you need? How do you even know what they are? You were on the right track when you raided the library and came home with your car loaded with books on time management, personnel management, fiscal management, and organizational management. You were on the right track when you picked up the application for a management training program.

There is no lack of available material and educational programs to teach you everything you ever wanted to know about "management." The bad news is that management is not the same as leadership. It is one step down from the top, which is where *you* want to be.

Confusing management and leadership is easy. They look alike: being in charge. But distinguishing between the two means that you can properly train for both (pausing ever so temporarily at management on your way to the top). Management is how an order is carried out. Leadership is why the order was there in the first place. Leading is good. You want to be a *leader.*

Learning to Lead

Getting the education and experience you need as a leader is not as easy as for a manager. *The Military Review* (reading material for

U.S. Army generals) characterizes leadership as "one of the most observed and least understood phenomena on earth." But the qualities that define a leader are elusive, and even if you could pinpoint some of them, they would be difficult to claim as your own.

Take "courage," for example. We all agree that courage is one of the qualities of an effective leader, but agreeing is vastly different from being able to add it to your list of personal qualities. You have to find courage in yourself, develop it carefully, harness it effectively, and use it wisely. But how?

Take heart. Experts agree that most of the qualities of leadership can indeed be taught. If you're the right person—one who has decided to lead—you *can* learn. You need a teacher.

So who did I choose to guide you through the labyrinth of contemporary leadership theories? Who is eminently qualified to interpret the emerging organizational paradigms, modern leadership technologies, breakthrough MBA curricula, cutting-edge *Fortune 500* programs, groundbreaking human resources philosophies, and personal growth jargon?

Benjamin Franklin, that's who! The man who will put 250 years of experience into your resume!

I know what you're thinking. You're thinking that, although Benjamin Franklin was indisputably the greatest American statesman, author, and businessman of the 18th century, what could a guy who's been dead for a couple of hundred years possibly teach us about leadership in modern times? If we study the principles of this motto-spouting curmudgeon, we'll miss out on all the latest stuff. Our information will be outmoded, and we won't be able to compete—much less lead—in the fast-paced workplace of today. We'll be hobbling around in powdered wigs and reciting a lot of homespun homilies like "Early to bed, early to rise makes a man healthy, wealthy, and wise."

WRONG! I assure you that no one is more qualified to ignite the leader within you than Benjamin Franklin. Not only was his own career red hot, he also really understood how to respond when things around him were heating up. He was the "Father of Firefighting"—the man who founded the first volunteer fire department and developed fire insurance as we know it.

Benjamin Franklin, born on January 17, 1706, clearly enjoyed being first. He was the first American diplomat, ambassador, storyteller, published scientist, postmaster general, inventor, and econo-mist. He organized the first lending library, the first medical center, the first scientific society, the first philosophical society, the first volunteer fire department, and the first fire insurance company. He invented the lightning rod, bifocals, the static electric generator, and the Franklin stove. He was the only American Founding Father who signed all four of the major documents that established American independence: the Declaration of Independence, the treaty with France, the treaty with England, and the Constitution. Not bad for a man who had only two years of formal education and was a dropout by age 10. Young Ben, in spite of his father's decision to cut his schooling short and consign him to apprenticeships for his training, embarked on a personal lifelong pursuit of self-educa-tion and self-improvement.

The results throughout his life were stunning. Not only did he edu-cate and improve himself, he also shared that knowledge as a prolific writer who just happened to own a print shop and could publish. His famous *Poor Richard's Almanac* is still a popular compendium of home-spun wisdom. As he developed his own philosophies and leadership style, he found ways to hone his skills and reap rich harvest. Early in his career as a printer in Philadelphia, he organized a group of neigh-borhood tradesmen into a "club of mutual improvement" called the Junto or the Leather-Apron Club. These men assembled every Friday evening to discuss how they could improve themselves and their com-munity. Membership in the Junto depended on the answers to four important questions establishing an attitude of leadership and a com-mitment to action:

1. Have you any particular disrespect of any present members?
   Answer: I have not.
2. Do you sincerely declare that you love mankind in general, of what profession or religion soever?
   Answer: I do.
3. Do you think any person ought to be harmed in his body, name, or goods for mere speculative opinions or his external way of worship?
   Answer: No.

4. Do you love truth for truth's sake, and will you endeavour impartially to find and receive it yourself and communicate it to others?

    Answer: I will.

There were then 24 questions to be answered at every meeting. Examples included: "Do you know of any fellow citizen who has lately done a worthy action, deserving praise and imitation?" "Do you know of any fellow citizen who has committed an error proper for us to be warned against and avoid?" "Do you think of anything at present in which the Junto may be serviceable to mankind, to their country, to their friends, or to themselves?" "Do you know of any deserving young beginner lately set up who it lies in the power of the Junto any way to encourage?"

The Junto's activities were not limited to discussions and answering questions. There was real action. From the Junto came the library, medical center, fire department, fire insurance company, and school, as well as urban projects such as the city watch and street paving, lighting, and cleaning. The seeds of leadership took deep root in Ben's life.

Franklin Still Delivers

Benjamin Franklin is a master who still delivers an ageless study in leadership basics—ideas and methods that have endured and are as true today as they were nearly 300 years ago. Although technologies have advanced since the 1700s, and buzzwords and sound bites have spiced up our workplace vocabulary, very little has actually changed—especially human nature. The fundamental principles of leadership developed by Benjamin Franklin are the foundation for business practices as we know them today. Best of all, they are refreshingly simple and easy to understand.

In this book, we'll take the most sophisticated leadership principles and run them through the wringer. We'll translate them into simple English. We'll filter them through the no-nonsense sensibilities of Benjamin Franklin. Finally, we'll see how those leadership principles have worked in the lives of successful men and women as they share their stories and advice with you. The result will be a 250-year perspective on leadership in its essence for you to enjoy.

Franklin, even though he educated himself, recognized that self-education is not the best way to learn. He himself once wrote, "He that teaches himself hath a fool for a master." Learning is much faster when you have teachers, especially good ones. Together, Ben Franklin and I will join forces with recognized experts to bring you the skills you'll need to ignite the leader within you.

Lessons Franklin Learned in Making New Year's Resolutions

Benjamin Franklin's many professional accomplishments and personal triumphs were not accidental. He clearly understood both management and leadership. More importantly, he understood that he must learn to lead himself before he could effectively lead other people. It is a wise lesson that any aspiring leader would do well to note, and it is where we will start your training.

At 25, with all the bravado and optimism of youth, Benjamin Franklin proclaimed for himself a "bold and arduous project," the purpose of which was "arriving at moral perfection." To that end, he drew up a list of 12 Resolutions and later added a 13th. He called them the Virtues. They served as a template for his life and could serve as a template for yours. They were:

1. *Temperance.* Eat not to dullness; drink not to elevation.
2. *Silence.* Speak not but what may benefit others or yourself; avoid trifling conversation.
3. *Order.* Let all your things have their places; let each part of your business have its time.
4. *Resolution.* Resolve to perform what you ought; perform without fail what you resolve.
5. *Frugality.* Make no expense but to do good to others or yourself; i.e., waste nothing.
6. *Industry.* Lose no time; be always employ'd in something useful; cut off all unnecessary actions.
7. *Sincerity.* Use no hurtful deceit; think innocently and justly, and if you speak, speak accordingly.
8. *Justice.* Wrong none by doing injuries or omitting the benefits that are your duty.
9. *Moderation.* Avoid extremes; forbear resenting injuries so much as you think they deserve.

10. *Cleanliness.* Tolerate no uncleanliness in body, clothes, or habitation.

11. *Tranquility.* Be not disturbed at trifles or at accidents common or unavoidable.

12. *Chastity.* Rarely use venery but for health or offspring, never to dullness, weakness, or the injury of your own or another's peace or reputation.

    and finally ...

13. *Humility.* (This is the very tall order Benjamin added later!) Imitate Jesus and Socrates.

Scholars today point out that Franklin's resolutions—the Virtues—are not all that unusual. Indeed, they sound vaguely biblical to me. What is truly unique was his plan to put them into effect. He admitted that his intention was to acquire the habitude of all these virtues. "I judg'd it would be well not to distract my attention by attempting the whole at once, but to fix on one of them at a time; and, when I should be master of that, then to proceed to another, and so on, till I should have gone thro' the thirteen."

Action in the Right Direction
Is the Key to Success

Franklin recognized that action—methodical steps toward mastering his Virtues—was the key to success. He wrote, "I concluded, at length, that the mere speculative conviction that it was our interest to be completely virtuous was not sufficient to prevent our slipping; and that the contrary habits must be broken, and good ones acquired and established, before we can have any dependence on a steady, uniform rectitude of conduct."

Merely wanting something to happen is not the same as making it happen. You have to take action, preferably daily. Otherwise, the resolution is only a dream. Warren Bennis, a distinguished professor of business administration at the University of Southern California and Pulitzer Prize-nominated author, quotes a business expert who was participating in one of his studies. The man told Bennis that the progress of his outfit was "a dream with a deadline." I really like that. Goals work the same way. In other words, if you want that dream to be a goal, *move*!

Keeping Score

Benjamin Franklin monitored his methodical mastery of the Virtues and carried a small book in which he kept score. He allocated one page for each Virtue and ruled the page with seven columns—creating one for each day of the week—in red ink. Then he crossed these columns with 13 red lines, creating one space for each of the 13 Virtues.

Figure 1

The Virtue Book

Form of the Pages
Temperance
Eat not to dullness; drink not to elevation

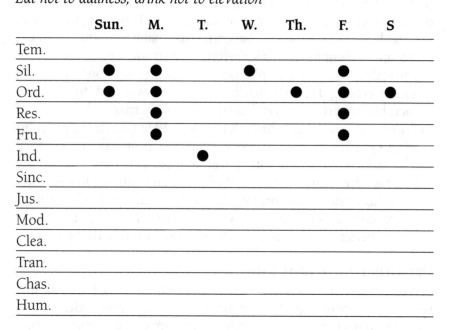

	Sun.	M.	T.	W.	Th.	F.	S
Tem.							
Sil.	●	●		●		●	
Ord.	●	●			●	●	●
Res.		●				●	
Fru.		●				●	
Ind.			●				
Sinc.							
Jus.							
Mod.							
Clea.							
Tran.							
Chas.							
Hum.							

When he failed to keep a Virtue, he would mark the page with a black mark for each day he failed. Remember, he tackled them one at a time. He assigned each Virtue a week during which he would give it his strictest attention. Because he was concentrating on only one at a time, he allowed the others to ordinary chance. If, for example, the week was devoted to Temperance, his goal was to keep the Temperance line free from black marks. If he succeeded for a week, then he concluded that the habit of Temperance had been strengthened. When he thought he had mastered a Virtue, he extended his attention to include an additional Virtue the following week and aspired to keep both lines clear. His goal was to have 13 weeks without one black mark.

If You Make a Mistake, Wipe Your Slate Clean and Try Again

Ben was surprised to find himself so much fuller of faults than he had imagined, but he did enjoy the satisfaction of seeing them diminish. Did he ever succeed in achieving perfection? Probably not. Although he never disclosed whether he actually achieved even one perfect 13-week mastery of all Virtues, we know that Franklin, like all of us, had a tough time keeping his resolutions. (Knowing this makes you feel better, doesn't it?) He lamented that "habit took the advantage of intention; inclination was sometimes too strong for reason."

A frugal fellow, Franklin planned to reuse his little book every 13 weeks by erasing the black marks and starting over. It didn't happen. In fact, his imperfection yielded so many black marks that he eventually erased holes right through the paper! He then transferred his scoring system to leaves of ivory, from which an offending pencil mark could be removed with a wet sponge. Ben Franklin literally wiped his slate clean after a round of personal failures. I like to think that he understood the importance of forgiving yourself for your transgressions and moving on (without black marks against you) to try to do better. You never know when you'll eventually succeed.

Put Order Into Your Life

While pursuing his Virtues, Ben Franklin evolved into our first time-management expert. His intention was to infuse order (Virtue No. 3) into his life so that he could move from one personal and professional pursuit to another, giving each the time, energy, and focus it required to be successful. He designated one page of his little ivory book to enter his 24-hour master schedule. As he did with all of his Virtues, he first made note of a perfectly ordered day and then kept score to see how close he could come to adhering to his plan. He said, "Every part of my business should have its allotted time."

Figure 2

Franklin's Daily Schedule

The precept of *Order* requiring that *every part of my business should have its allotted time,* one page in my little book contain'd the following scheme of employment for the twenty-four hours of a natural day.

THE MORNING	5	Rise, wash, and address
Question. What good		Powerful Goodness! Contrive
shall I do this day?	6	day's business, and take the
		resolution of the day;
	7	prosecute the present study,
		and breakfast.
	8	
	9	
	10	Work.
	11	

NOON	12	Read, or overlook my
	1	accounts, and dine.
	2	
	3	Work.
	4	
	5	

EVENING	6	Put things in their places.
Question. What good	7	Supper. Music or diversion,
have I done	8	or conversation. Examination
to-day?	9	of the day.

NIGHT	10	
	11	
	12	
	1	Sleep.
	2	
	3	
	4	

Franklin was the first to admit that, as his career flourished, it was not possible for his perfectly ordered schedule to be "exactly observed by a master, who must mix with the world, and often receive people of business at their own hours." He acknowledged that things happen in the course of a busy day that require flexibility. But the value of examining how you spend your time and, more importantly, how you don't spend it, could yield some interesting information.

In pursuit of order, Franklin aspired to neaten up more than time. He noted that everything has its time and place. So he extended his tidiness to things (he specifically mentions paper) as well. Although he left no specific instructions for methodically cleaning out drawers or bulldozing off the top of a desk, he did leave us with the certainty that we'll get more done if we don't have to waste time hunting for things. (You'll notice that his daily schedule allots no time for "hunting for all the stuff I lose.")

Lead Yourself First

When, like Benjamin Franklin, you can lead yourself by setting goals, evaluating your weaknesses and strengths, planning, and taking action when you know the time is right, then you begin to understand the nature of leadership. You're ready to ignite the leader within.

PERSONAL STUDY EXERCISES

1. Use your experience in writing New Year's resolutions as a spring-board for leadership.

We all make New Year's resolutions, and we all break them. We all vow to do better next year. Okay, we all admit that making New Year's resolutions is usually an exercise in futility. Researchers report that the most common resolution in the United States is to lose weight. Logic would suggest that, by every February, we should be a nation of skinny, happy people. Yet it's never happened. Ever. Like Ben Franklin, we allow our bad habits to override our good intentions. So, if we are incapable of keeping one simple resolution, why then don't we abandon the practice altogether and embrace another, less humiliating tradition that doesn't annually remind us of how weak-willed we are? Because, like Ben, we are all optimistic and instinctively recognize that making New Year's resolutions is the way we learn to:

Set our sights on what we want. (This is as far as most of us get.)
Evaluate our strengths and weaknesses.
Plan our steps for getting from where we are to where we want to be.
Take action.

Remember, concocting a resolution is not the way to bring change into your life. Success is achieved only when you take all of the steps. I'm going to add a new step to our collective tradition: Keep a notebook like Benjamin Franklin's. Simply shifting from *thinking about* doing something to *doing* something instantly transforms your list from resolutions (meant to be broken) into goals (meant to be pursued with a vengeance). I don't need to remind you that lists of resolutions can be made *anytime*. You don't need to wait until New Year's Eve when you're sipping champagne, listening to Guy Lombardo's Orchestra, and deflecting hails of confetti. I suggest that you get yourself a yellow pad *right now*.

Make a list. Give each goal—or Virtue—its own page and particular attention. (Because we are talking about developing leadership here, I am using a career-oriented goal as an example, but you could develop goals for any aspect of your life. The steps are the same.)

Set your sights on what you want. Specify in detail where you want to be in your career. What's your goal? When do you want to achieve it?

Evaluate your weaknesses and strengths. Why have you not already achieved your goal? What are the personal, professional, and circumstantial weaknesses that have impeded you from achieving it? What are the strengths you bring to the equation? What do you already have and already know that will help you get to where you want to be?

Plan your steps for getting from where you are to where you want to be. Starting right now, what can you do step by step and day by day to achieve this goal? For example, do you need to take classes, change departments, network with other people who are doing the job you want, tell your boss you want to enter the management track program, lose weight, take extra time with your appearance, or move to another city?

Take action. What one action can you take right this minute to put you on the path toward achievement? Do it. Nothing begets success like success. Moving toward your goal—even one small step—creates the momentum you need to signal your entire heart and soul that you are serious. This is happening, really happening.

Keep a notebook like Benjamin Franklin's. Keep score on your daily progress with a journal or a calendar. Make a move toward your goal every day and record it, or note when you have failed to make a move. Evaluate your failures, but forgive yourself for being less than perfect by ceremoniously erasing those black marks at intervals and giving yourself clean pages from which to work. In doing so, you'll learn to keep moving forward when things might not be going so well, and you'll see real progress.

Happy New Year! You're on your way!

2. Put order into thy calendar.

Do not rush out and buy a commercial time planner. You don't need one for this exercise. All you need is a yellow pad and brutal honesty. No one is looking but you! If you already have a commercial time planner but don't use it, this is a clear indication that you have wonderful intentions but slip on the follow-through. It's time to buckle down. Write that in the first available space under today's date. If you already have a commercial time planner and use it, congratulations. It will be useful as you examine your real use of hours.

A client once complained to me that he wanted to get in shape but he absolutely did *not* have enough time to get to the gym for one hour three times a week. If there was anyone who needed to work out, this was the man: middle aged, overweight, out of shape, stressed out, and a perfect candidate for a heart attack. Listening to his excuses, I then asked, "Are you willing to bet your life that you haven't got the time?" He flinched almost imperceptibly but stuck to his guns. "That's right, Mike. I haven't got the time." I handed him a yellow pad and a pen and said, "Okay, show me how you use your time." He scrawled:

Wake up, shower, dress, breakfast—1 hour
Drive to office—30 minutes
Work—9 hours
Drive home—30 minutes
Dinner with family—30 minutes
Sleep—8 hours

He shoved the pad toward me and said, "Look, Mike. Sleep. Eat. Work. No time!" I nodded and then took out my calculator, did some quick math, then pointed out, "Your daily schedule adds up to 19 hours and 30 minutes. There are 24 hours in a day. That means you've got 4 hours and 30 minutes every day when apparently you're not doing anything. That's 22 hours and 30 minutes during the workweek. We haven't even looked at your weekends yet. I figure that gives you another 48 hours. According to my calculations, you could swing by the gym three times a week for an hour each time and still have 67 hours and 30 minutes left over. Am I missing something here?"

Right there, he took out his calendar and made some appointments for himself to go to the gym. Why had he not done so before? Either he really thought he didn't have enough time because his perception of time was distorted or, more likely, he simply didn't want to go. Clearing both hurdles was important to get him to move. When he saw his schedule laid out in black and white, the truth was indisputable, the conclusion obvious. Get thee to the gym, lazy man! Just as Ben Franklin noted, "Contrary habits must be broken, and good ones acquired and established."

My client is still going to the gym and is doing great.

Let's Franklinize Your Schedule

First, get a yellow pad and a pen. Divide your life into two types of days: workdays and nonworkdays. Select *two* of each type to study. Make certain that the days you select are typical. They don't need to be sequential. Next, organize a sheet of yellow pad paper into a time study sheet, or photocopy the time study sheet below and use it.

Figure 3

The Time Study Sheet

Midnight	Activity	Noon	Activity
12:00–12:15		12:00–12:15	
12:15–12:30		12:15–12:30	
12:30–12:45		12:30–12:45	
12:45–1:00		12:45–1:00	
1:00–1:15		1:00–1:15	
1:15–1:30		1:15–1:30	
1:30–1:45		1:30–1:45	
1:45–2:00		1:45–2:00	
2:00–2:15		2:00–2:15	
2:15–2:30		2:15–2:30	
2:30–2:45		2:30–2:45	
2:45–3:00		2:45–3:00	
3:00–3:15		3:00–3:15	
3:15–3:30		3:15–3:30	
3:30–3:45		3:30–3:45	
3:45–4:00		3:45–4:00	
4:00–4:15		4:00–4:15	
4:15–4:30		4:15–4:30	

Midnight	Activity	Noon	Activity
4:30–4:45		4:30–4:45	
4:45–5:00		4:45–5:00	
5:00–5:15		5:00–5:15	
5:15–5:30		5:15–5:30	
5:30–5:45		5:30–5:45	
5:45–6:00		5:45–6:00	
6:00–6:15		6:00–6:15	
6:15–6:30		6:15–6:30	
6:30–6:45		6:30–6:45	
6:45–7:00		6:45–7:00	
7:00–7:15		7:00–7:15	
7:15–7:30		7:15–7:30	
7:30–7:45		7:30–7:45	
7:45–8:00		7:45–8:00	
8:00–8:15		8:00–8:15	
8:15–8:30		8:15–8:30	
8:30–8:45		8:30–8:45	
8:45–9:00		8:45–9:00	
9:00–9:15		9:00–9:15	
9:15–9:30		9:15–9:30	
9:30–9:45		9:30–9:45	
9:45–10:00		9:45–10:00	
10:00–10:15		10:00–10:15	
10:15–10:30		10:15–10:30	
10:30–10:45		10:30–10:45	
10:45–11:00		10:45–11:00	
11:00–11:15		11:00–11:15	
11:15–11:30		11:15–11:30	
11:30–11:45		11:30–11:45	
11:45–12:00		11:45–12:00	

For each of the four days (two work and two nonwork), record every activity (including telephone calls) in 15-minute blocks. Be honest! If the day suddenly goes nuts—you wake up with appendicitis, or nine cousins show up unexpectedly from Kansas—ditch the time study and select another day. You'll learn nothing from documenting an odd day except that life happens.

At the conclusion of your study, take a close, hard, brutally honest look at how you're really spending your time. Use a calculator if necessary. You might find it interesting to categorize your time expenditures, such as "working" and "eating."

Now, put it all together.

— Examine your goals.
— Examine the daily steps you determined would further your goals.
— Design an *ideal* day that gives you time to meet all your obligations and yet leaves room for moving in the direction of your goals.
— Contrast your *real* day against your IDEAL day. After you finish rolling on the floor with laughter, decide where you are going wrong. Identify the time thieves and wasters. Get rid of them.

Now, design a BEN FRANKLIN day—one that balances reality with ideal scheduling. Take out your calendar and put that day into the schedule *tomorrow.* And like Ben Franklin, keep score. Make notes for yourself on where you failed to meet your own expectations and why. Give yourself huge points for being able to adhere to your plan. The closer you come to controlling your days, the closer you'll come to an ordered life.

Finally, in the spirit of Ben and his quest for total order, go clean out a drawer. Do it now.

CHAPTER 2

Becoming a Born Leader

"Life is a kind of chess, in which we have often points to gain, and competitors or adversaries to contend with, and in which there is a vast variety of good and ill events. By playing at chess, then we may learn."
—Ben Franklin

Leadership is difficult to define. Yet, even without definition, we all recognize leadership. It's a complex amalgam of qualities that make one person powerful enough to cause the whole to exceed the sum of its parts. In other words, a leader's true power is not so much in what he can do but what he can get other people to do. A Chinese proverb wisely says, "A good leader is one whom people respect. The poor leader is one whom people hate. But the great leader is one who, when the people have finished, they say 'we have done it ourselves.' "

John Gardner, scholar, author, counselor to six American presidents and founder of Common Cause, writes, "The notion that all the attributes of a leader are innate is demonstrably false. No doubt certain characteristics are genetically determined—level of energy, for example. But the individual's hereditary gifts, however notable, leave the issue of future leadership performance undecided, to be settled by later events and influences."

There's no such thing as a born leader. Leadership can't be taught, but it can be learned. Let's get started.

How Leaders Are Trained in the Workplace

In the past, all major corporations developed educational programs to train their leaders. They ran the gamut from simple home-study materials to full-blown corporate universities with campuses, courses, and faculty. No matter how big or small the programs, they were all focused on building competencies and skills selected to meet the companies' requirements. But the programs were not yielding the results that had been expected. Certainly, they were graduating good managers with specific skills, but good managers could only take the companies so far. To be really successful, companies needed leaders with broad-based knowledge and experience. Scale was one problem with developmental programs. The larger the company, the larger the program. The larger the program, the less likely it was to be suited to an individual. Developmental programs were, after all, designed to train a lot of people—it was easy to train managers this way. Far more difficult was training leaders. They discovered that leadership, not management, is critical to the success of a dynamic organization. Today, the direction of training has changed. Instead of the old methodical basics, employees are more likely to find self-directed learning that helps them look for ways to sharpen their own knowledge, develop the ability to access information, and learn more quickly and efficiently.

The way we train people in emergency services closely mirrors the old style of corporate leadership development. We build specific competencies and skills at each stage of our careers. You're probably being trained this way. Just before you assume new responsibilities, you're trained to perform the necessary skills. Mastery is up to you and comes later with experience. Methodically training skill-by-skill right before you need each one is undeniably efficient, but it's also halting. You don't rise through the ranks so much as plod uphill one step at a time, hesitating before each step. While this style of development gives you the tools you need to do your job well and can even train you to be a manager or supervisor, it rarely develops *leadership*. You'll have to do *that* on your own.

How the Experts Describe the Qualities, Attributes, and Skills of a Leader

Thousands have tried to define leadership and describe leaders. Here are three expert points of view for you to consider. The United States Army has identified qualities that combined define a leader:

versatility,

adaptability to change,

professionalism,

exemplary ethical conduct,

technical and tactical proficiency,

great communication skills,

ability to build cohesive teams,

analytical problem-solving skills,

willingness to seize initiative,

independence and confidence to operate with minimal guidance, and

insight and foresight of a visionary.

William Bennis, author of *On Becoming a Leader*, writes, "All leaders share guiding vision, passion, integrity, trust, curiosity, and daring." He also assures us that "although intelligence and certain personality traits facilitate the transformation into leader, most skills can be learned."

Organizational expert Robert Katz says that leaders rely on three basic skills:

Technical skill. Specialized knowledge in one's field and enough experience to analyze and apply that knowledge.

Human skill. The ability to work with people individually and in teams.

Conceptual skill. The ability to see your organization as a whole and promote performance that will advance the common good.

The Truth About Leadership

Although leadership theories are many and the definitions can be quite complex, I want to tell you a secret: Everyone is a leader. Some are just better than others. We all have our own road maps and choose our own routes. When one person is given authority and designated as the "leader," he or she "reigns first among equals." No one can lead you unless you decide to follow. When you decide to follow, you *give* another person authority. It's *your* decision, *your* gift.

Leadership, on any level, is a simple matter of consensus. When you stand up and say "Follow me!" remember that the person you're recruiting is also a leader. For him to give you the authority to lead, that person has to believe that your value system, mission, and strategy are in perfect agreement with his own. Then and only then will he allow you to take control, and allow you to maintain that control only so long as you do nothing to violate your consensus. Literally, the leader in you has to become partners with the leader in him.

Remember back when you were a little kid and you did something really awful and got caught? While your mom was yelling at you, you whined something like, "It wasn't my fault! Charles made me do it!" And your mom asked that standard question *all* moms ask and *all* kids hate to hear: "If Charles told you to jump off a bridge, would you do it?!?" And you said, "Uh, no ...." Even as children, we *choose* leaders. There's no more clear demonstration of your absolute need to come to consensus with someone and give him authority than putting the decision to the old "If Charles told you to jump off a bridge, would you do it?" test. If you followed Charles into one bad-kid act, it was *your* choice. The act was entirely consistent with your values. You decided to lead yourself to follow Charles. If Charles had then told you to jump off a bridge, this mandate would have been inconsistent with your values, and the leader within you would have taken control. Of course, you wouldn't have jumped. No one can *make* you do anything you don't *want* to do, *ever*. You have to agree to do it. You have to arrive at consensus.

Leadership Doesn't Have to Be Good

When human resources experts discuss developing leadership, they generally focus on the best that leadership can be, defining leadership in terms of the highest ideals and laying out plans for training pillars and paragons. Because leadership is simple consensus, it's entirely possible for leadership to be evil. Adolf Hitler, for example, was unquestionably an effective leader. He stood up and said, "Follow me!" Then he submitted his value system, mission, and strategy to followers who weighed his offerings. They all had to come to a consensus. They all had to decide that they agreed with him. They had to *give* him the authority to lead, and they had to choose to follow. The leaders in them had to become partners with the leader in Hitler. Their collective value system, mission, and strategy were horribly wrong, but all of the people involved were in agreement, and Hitler was the leader.

The point is to make sure that you understand that leadership is neither good nor evil. Leadership is consensus. However, if you're going to lead, you'd better be good. When you're good, you attract better followers.

The wise and often-quoted Chinese leader Confucius learned much of what he knew about leadership from the guide I Ching. It says, "Radical changes require adequate authority. A man must have inner strength as well as influential position. What he does must correspond with a higher truth. If the revolution is not founded on such inner truth, the results are bad, and it has no success. For in the end, men will support only those undertakings which they feel instinctively to be just."

You'll Never Be Promoted to Leadership

Knowing that leadership is a simple matter of consensus between you and those who choose to follow you, you now know that someone from the top of your organization can't walk in and designate you as the leader. Not even promotion to the highest rank will make you the leader. Designation and promotion *will* make you the manager of the organization. Being leader is something very, very different.

Before you get discouraged, realize that, although you can't be promoted to leader, it's entirely possible that you can be a leader of people before you're ever promoted. In fact, you might be that kind of leader already. (The mere fact that you're reading this is a good indicator!) Remember that leadership is a consensus that you will be given permission to reign first among equals. For this reason, leadership can emerge anytime in your career when that consensus is reached between you and people who follow your lead. Indeed, in every company, there are employees who are low in the ranks but to whom everyone instinctively turns for direction. They are the gyroscopes that keep the group on kilter. These are the people who truly lead in spite of the formal organizational chart, where rank and file have designated other people to call the shots.

For example, if you're out on a call and a supervisor issues an order, you (no matter what your rank) will consider the order and decide whether it's consistent with what you believe to be right. If it is, your leader within says, "Okay, I agree with him. I'll do it." If it isn't, your leader within says, "No way. I think he's off base. I'm not going to do it." I guarantee you that you search for consensus every single time someone attempts to assert authority over you. You must come to a consensus before you move. Now, if you happen to be the leader in your group, when the order comes down from the supervisor and you make your decision to obey or disobey, then others will follow your lead. If you were to turn to your coworkers and say, "The supervisor is trying to get us all killed. I can't do what he asked," you would not be alone in your decision to disobey the order. This is how consensus works. It has nothing to do with the supervisor.

Factors in Your Favor Already

Fortunately, as a person working in emergency services, you already have a number of built-in good leadership attributes. Researchers identified these attributes while studying physicians who made the transition from clinical practices to administration. These specific attributes apply not only to physicians but to anyone who works in emergency services on any level.

You're credible. You have a solid reputation for trustworthiness built on an excellent personal track record. You've worked for a long time, done a good job, and have demonstrated dependability that people count on. On and off the job, people rely on you to do the right thing and tell the truth.

You're in great shape. Working in emergency services demands that you be in great shape physically, mentally, and emotionally. You're not allowed to walk off the scene of an accident just because you get pooped or decide that you've had enough. No, you're trained to raise your capacity for strain and discomfort to the highest levels and sustain them until your job is done. You've developed extraordinary endurance and resilience through your work.

You're willing to take responsibility for people's lives. The very nature of emergency services is that of taking responsibility and control. You walk into chaos and restore order. That's your job. But it's more than that. You also know the feeling of holding another person's life in your hands. You have the courage to make those difficult decisions that will affect the outcome of potentially fatal circumstances.

You know how to listen and interpret nonverbal cues. You have spent years evaluating patients who couldn't tell you everything you needed to know before you treated them. You have developed a finely tuned ability to read all sorts of signals to make accurate diagnoses and assessments. Although you are a great listener, you don't need to rely on what people say to get the full picture. Not only are you able to quickly and accurately gather information, you're also able to pick it up from several sources simultaneously and put it all together into a comprehensive understanding of the situation.

You know how to deal with crises. Because your stock in trade is disaster management, you know how to stay absolutely calm when everyone around you is panicking. You have learned to get your emotions under control in situations that unnerve the average person. You have learned to be objective about your personal safety and to take calculated risks without succumbing to personal fear. More than that, you are able to transmit confidence to other people with your calm demeanor.

You know how to deal with people. You're in a profession that allows you to see people at their very best and their very worst. You're privileged to great comedies and terrible tragedies of life. When you're called in, you're in control, so you know how to deal with them to ensure their comfort and safety no matter how difficult the circumstances. You have had to tell people bad news, comfort the sick and dying, and share joy and relief. Because of your experience, you know people very well.

Even With All of This, the Transition to Formal Leadership Won't Be Easy

Before you go skipping off to claim your rightful throne, be advised that a background in emergency services also produces some serious impediments—areas of difficulty in leadership that stem directly from your training in the profession. These are problems that you have to overcome before you can be a good leader.

You're used to being independent. While it's true that you've spent your career working on a team of people under the direction of supervisors, you'll have to admit that, in the final analysis, you call the shots. For example, if you're out on a rescue call to assist with a person injured in a car wreck, *you* do the patient evaluation, *you* make the diagnosis, *you* decide the treatment, and *you* open the kits. You might be accompanied by other rescue personnel, and you might be following protocol and procedures set by other people, but *you* are the one who is ultimately responsible. Emergency service doesn't wait for committee meetings. *You* have to move, *on your own*, in a split second. On the other hand, leadership requires that you accomplish the missions of your organization by relying on the efforts of other people. It can mean a tough adjustment in thinking.

You've never focused on the organization as a whole. To the point that you step up into leadership, your focus is on you and your buddies. It's natural, because you need to pay attention to the tasks at hand. Indeed, you have work to do every minute of every day. You pay little attention to anyone above or below you unless their actions directly affect you and your tasks. In fact, you're aware of nothing they do unless you're directly involved. This "keep your head down and nose to the grindstone" mentality serves you well, dutiful one. Up to this point, it's made you efficient. But when you step into leadership, you have to broaden your view. Suddenly *everything* is your business: upside, downside, inside, and outside.

You're not skilled in organizational dynamics. Right now, you're task-oriented and accustomed to following orders and completing assignments. Also, you work in an organization that places clear divisions between administration and employees. Consequently, you've had little exposure to the intricate and secret inner workings that make the company tick. There is a huge difference between being able to work within the organization and understanding how it all fits together. It's sort of like flying with a friend. Being the frequent passenger in the copilot's seat of a small aircraft doesn't qualify you to land it. You might understand the basic principles of flight. You might be familiar with all of the gauges and levers. You might have taken over the controls in an exciting moment closely supervised by your pilot friend. But you are not qualified to land. Got it? It's the same with organizations. Leading an organization (well) is harder than it looks.

You don't have all of the skills you need. I have a friend who breezed through college rather easily and went right into graduate school. But graduate school wasn't as great as she thought it would be. She remarked that she had mistakenly assumed that the graduate program would be just more of the same course work she had taken as an undergraduate, just more advanced. Her dismay was that the courses were not only advanced, they were different. The higher up in her program she progressed, the worse it became. By the time she got to her doctorate, she was having to take such courses as dissertation writing and statistics—subjects entirely out of her field but necessary to her graduate curriculum. You'll find the same challenge in leadership. As you step up, you can be assured that your world will not only be advanced but different. Leadership isn't a matter of doing more of the same things you've always done in bigger and better versions. Leadership requires all that, plus additional skills.

You aren't used to persuading. Most emergency services organizations are "command cultures" based on the military model. "Command culture" means that superior officers give orders to people of lower rank who follow them—there's little or no discussion. Someone commands and someone obeys. Because that's the culture you know best, you're accustomed to ordering what you want done. Once you've done that, you have every reason to believe that the person to whom you issued the order will execute it exactly as you commanded. It's easy to confuse your authority with leadership. Just because you have the authority to bark an order and get a person to move doesn't mean you're leading. On the contrary, you're just passing along an order you got when you were handed the authority of rank. Leading requires that you persuade rather than control. Persuasion is the fine art of give and take. You listen to the other person's point of view, decide together to work for the good of your common mission, construct your strategy, and move forward. You respect the other person's intelligence and experience enough to engage his cooperation. You lead.

You like being one of the gang. One of the most difficult transitions you'll make in your professional life is that step up to leader. It instantly separates you from the comfortable, congenial company of your colleagues and isolates you in an unfamiliar world of authority and responsibility. For most, the transition is a welcome one and one for which the preparation has been thorough. But even the easiest transition is a wrenching experience for you and everyone around you. One minute you're their buddy and the next minute you're the boss. No one knows how to act around you. You're not entirely comfortable with sudden authority. There's resentment and jealousy among the people you left behind. Even good-natured kidding masks uncertainty about where your relationships will go now. How can you remain friends when you have the authority to fire them? How can they respect your authority when they've seen your faults and failures up close? If you think it's lonely at the top and not worth the effort, you're wrong. It's not lonely. In fact, it gives you more access to people. And it's very worth the effort. There's a saying among dogsled mushers: "The lead dog always gets frost on his nose, but his view is better." If you'll remember that leadership is a lifelong evolution of human development, then you'll realize that you don't have to know everything from the get-go. Because all of your buddies know you have faults, you don't have to hold up a facade of perfection. As for leaving buddies behind, don't. You're all still in this together. Never forget where you came from, because in a sense, that's still where you are. It's the foundation on which you will build an informed, sensitive organizational culture.

Leadership by Getting Out of the Way

Hewlett-Packard, well known in the world for innovative leadership development, manages many of its projects with an unexpected and effective method known as "leadership by getting out of the way." Their team leaders get everyone working on the same mission but don't interfere with how the work gets done. This is where consensus is dynamically and powerfully directed to a common goal. Here's how it works: Team leaders don't have any of the traditional trophies of management. No fancy offices with mahogany desks and plush carpet. No authority to hire, evaluate, fire, or raise pay. What they do have is a consensus. The function of the team leaders is to keep the projects on track by allowing the team members to do what they do best—lead themselves. Of course, leaders have certain attributes and qualities that make them effective. For instance, they mirror the lists of defining behaviors that have been developed by leadership development experts. Among the behaviors are:

planning and organizational skills,
problem-solving skills,
the ability to bring order to chaos,

good communication skills—both one-on-one and in groups,
the ability to manage more than one thing at a time,
the ability to motivate team members,
security,
maturity,
humor,
willingness to delegate,
generosity, and
the ability to deal with conflict.

When a team leader assumes leadership, he behaves in ways that create a culture of safety. When the team members relax in this supportive environment, they know that their own leadership is respected and that there is an ongoing initiative toward a consensus. As for the team leader, "Respect is earned not by what the teacher knows but what the teacher is able to stimulate others to know." Team members are allowed to spread their wings with the leader's full support. They have assurance that the team leader will not slip into the less effective role of "manager." There won't come a moment when the team leader issues a command out of the blue and then waits for the members to scurry to obey. The mission doesn't belong to the team leader, it belongs to the whole team—they're equals. Is it effective? You bet. Not only is the work excellent, but everyone on the team develops finely tuned leadership abilities and behaviors. Hewlett-Packard is a powerful organization in more ways than one and getting more so every day!

Turning Your Organization Upside Down

As I said, the traditional management style of emergency services is a military command culture. Early fire departments and emergency services organizations were the domains of men and women who had been trained by the U.S. armed forces, which taught them that high-ranking officers give marching orders to the low-ranking soldiers, who obey immediately and without question. Familiar order and discipline were supremely important: shined shoes, pressed uniforms, rules, regulations, and cots so tightly covered that you could bounce quarters off of the blankets.

It is still much the same. If you doubt the parallels between the military and emergency services, notice that we still use the vocabulary of the military: platoon, squad, drill, and combat team. We still rank our men and women with military designations: lieutenant, captain, division commander, and battalion chief. We still wear spit-and-polish uniforms, follow orders, and rise through the ranks until we are on top. When we draw the organizational chart of our traditional workplace, we put the chief at the top and everyone else somewhere underneath. The lower the rank, the lower the slot on the chart. When it's finished, it's a giant pyramid. It's a pretty slick way to get the lay of the land and to see where people fit in.

The problem is that it's upside down. When you're the leader, you would do well to flip it over and get it right. Like the teams at Hewlett-Packard, you need to get crystal clear on just who works for whom.

When we envision leading and following, we mistakenly assume that "leading" is moving out in front and "following" is bringing up the rear. While this might be true when you ride your horse into battle with your troops marching behind you, in reality the act of leading is most effective when you get *behind* your followers. Your job is to create a workplace culture that is so safe and supportive that they can do their best. To do this, you have to work for them.

Working Your Way to the Bottom of the Organization

Certainly, no one wants to work his way to the bottom. But that is, in fact, what leaders should be doing, modifying at least one aspect of our military tradition of command culture. Simply by inverting the outmoded pyramid and poising it on its sharp point, you'll have a much more workable organization. The leader, now on the bottom, serves and supports high-level management, who in turn serves and supports middle management, who in turn serves and supports the members in the trenches every day, doing the job that we all work together to accomplish—serving the community by providing emergency services. Each segment, as it aligns nearer the top of our inverted pyramid, is larger in scope and scale, more visible, increasingly responsible for direct contact with the community, and in greater physical danger. Understandably, the "top" should feel uncomfortable. And, maybe in the past those people did—when they were following marching orders from people who were out of touch. But when people in every segment, especially the top, feel support and encouragement from the segments beneath them, then those people are more effective and their work performance is better.

If you want to lead and work for the people in your organization, you don't have to announce a major upheaval. No one needs to scramble to the copy machine with new organizational charts. You merely need to make a small personal attitude adjustment by reminding yourself just who works for whom in your organization. Once you are clear about the new chain of command, you need to take better care of the people you serve. Find out what they need in order to do their jobs, then make it happen.

A rewarding, gratifying by-product of the inverted pyramid management model is that you will be developing confident, competent, experienced leadership all the way to the top. Your upper level will be well prepared to work their way down to your level as they recognize you to be the leader they would one day like to be.

PERSONAL STUDY EXERCISES

1. Think about the last time someone "made" you do something you didn't want to do. Knowing now that you had to come to a consensus and agree to do it, what were the reasons you relented and complied?

2. Make a list of people for whom you work. (This is a trick question.) Write yourself a new job description that clearly defines what you do for them that allows them to do their jobs well.

3. Name a person you respect and follow. What qualities, values, attributes, or skills does the person have that are exactly like your own and that bring you to consensus? Is there anyone around who views you the same way?

CHAPTER 3

Climbing the Ladder of Success

"Moderate your desire of victory over your adversary, and be pleased with one over yourself."

—Ben Franklin

You're going places! All you have to do is work hard and meet certain very specific skill requirements, and you'll climb right up that ladder of success in the department! You won't have to compete with outsiders for those precious few promotions that become available when you're so ready that you're frothing to claim one for your own. Your organization promotes from within, so you've always got the inside track. Being on the inside means that the administration can help you get ready for every test, and better than that, you don't even have to prove yourself. After all, they know you and what you can do! Life doesn't get better—or worse—than this.

The Bright Side of Being on the Inside

In emergency services, there is precedent and protocol for everything that goes on, including procedures for promotion. From where you stand, you can easily see exactly where you want to go in the organization because each position is clearly defined by rank, and each rank is clearly defined by specific requirements. If you want to advance in the ranks, it's a simple matter of passing exams, demonstrating competencies, and lasting long enough to be promoted.

Fortunately, the organization expects you to work toward promotion and does several things to help you get there. First, most of the skills you need to advance are taught on the job. Second, things that are tricky are explained in books and study guides that are always available to you. Third, your job is unique in the workforce in that it provides blocks of downtime. Instead of watching TV between calls, you can study or practice skills at work. Unlike ambitious employees in the private sector, you won't have to put in a lot of personal time to get ahead. This is especially useful if you're a volunteer and your time is limited by a "real" job.

In addition to having easy access to a clear promotion track, you have the benefit of being familiar with the facilities, equipment, organization, and people who work there. Without question, the learning curve for an insider is considerably shorter than that of someone who is recruited from another organization and can't find the copy machine without a trail of bread crumbs. He has to start from scratch on nearly every aspect of simple functioning, and getting up to speed with just the basics can be agonizingly slow. Also, the administration knows you. They are the people who will be considering you for promotion. They've seen your work and know what you can do. Finally, your coworkers know what you know and who you are. They know what to expect.

The Dark Side of Being on the Inside

Almost all of the above. Let's take them one at a time.

In emergency services, there is precedent and protocol for everything that goes on, including promotion procedures. This might be efficient for the organization, but it doesn't allow for the sudden emergence of a shining star. There's very little room for creative innovations such as the development of new programs and divisions where you can step in and take over. In the private sector, corporations invent and reinvent themselves at the speed of light to accomplish their missions. But emergency services is a very different environment. Our organization must rely on restricted systems dictated by government; the nature of our interfaces with other agencies; and long traditions of neat, tidy divisions and stratifications in rank. Although creative people and innovative programs do exist in emergency services, nothing in our industry can compare with the private sector's ability to make independent decisions and take sweeping action. For example, if a private corporation decides that an executive is really talented in one particular area, the leadership can tap that talent by forming a whole new department for him and hiring a support staff to assist him—in a day. The sky's the limit. But this is never going to happen in emergency services. There aren't going to be any field promotions. No matter how good you are, you aren't going to be promoted without following the stringent protocols of the department. Fortunately, there is much you can do to prepare to be in the right place at the right time.

From where you stand, you can easily see exactly where you want to go in the organization because each position is clearly defined by rank, and each rank is clearly defined by specific requirements. Each rung on the ladder of success in your organization is clearly defined. You have a specific set of competencies and skills that serve you in your present position and keep you on your assigned step. The step above you has its own specific set of competencies and skills. Some are different from the ones you're using now, and some are merely advanced versions. *Before* you're allowed to step up the ladder, you have to have that new set. This sounds really good. But there's a problem. Frankly, you're getting the wrong idea about what it takes to lead. The acquisition of a newer, bigger bag of tricks is teaching you to be management—the interpreter of orders and the organizer of people to get the job done. This is a good thing for you. More authority, more prestige, and more money.

But remember, management is not leadership. Leadership is much, much more than a collection of skills and competencies. It's an elegant synthesis of personal attributes and qualities recognized and respected by people who choose to follow you.

There's one more difficulty with climbing the ladder rung by rung. It's a halting and slow ascent. There's no chance for a skyrocketing career. Besides, seeing the climb one step at a time keeps you focused on those things you don't know, and it allows you to be certain that the person above you knows only a little more. Keep your sights aimed *upward*, perhaps even *beyond* the rung of the ladder right above you. Work diligently to do and be the best you can, and trust that the people above you have done the same.

Most of the skills you need to advance are taught on the job. The first time you tackle a new skill, you'll likely fall flat on your face. No one is good at everything from the get-go. There are some skills that you'll master quickly because you have either natural talent or another related skill that makes the mastery of the new one easy. Still, for the most part, you can assume that a first encounter with something new will be difficult at best and downright disastrous at worst.

In emergency services, you learn new skills at work in a hands-on environment. Someone teaches you by using the equipment and materials that are available on the job. You can't learn to put out a deck fire on an aircraft carrier on your own because you don't have a flaming aircraft carrier at home. You'll have to do all of your stumbling and faltering in front of someone else—or a lot of people. No one likes to be embarrassed. You're at your present rank because you're demonstrably good at all of the competencies and skills that are required to achieve that rank. For one split second, you knew it all. You were on top of your game. But the minute you reached for the next rung of the ladder, you had to admit that you didn't have all of the answers—at least for the position you wanted. To get them, you have to acknowledge that you're deficient and, worse, you have to be willing to showcase every deficiency in the broad light of day in front of all of your buddies. It can be wrenching. You'll get reactions that range from raucous, good-natured ribbing to smug disdain. Your feelings might get hurt and your pride might be wounded.

Hurt feelings and wounded pride should be the least of your worries. There is a human tendency to shut down when we feel threatened. Little threatens a person more than being made to feel foolish. If you shut down, two things will happen. You'll make more mistakes, and you'll be less willing to take further risks. Enthusiasm, resolve, and a sincere desire to learn will quickly be replaced by the certainty that you are an idiot—just smart enough to know that you don't ever want to try *that* skill again.

People who teach you the new skills and competencies you'll need to advance probably aren't professional teachers. They're your buddies who were tapped to teach because they really knew how to do whatever it is that you're trying to learn. There is a huge difference between being able to *do* something and being able to teach it. Teaching is a highly skilled profession in itself. Although some people get lucky and are able to transmit information in a fairly understandable form, the majority are clueless about the elegant intricacies of teaching and learning. If you're a fortunate trainee, you'll be nestled under the wing of a person who has some innate sense of how to teach. When this doesn't happen, you'll be left coping with a new skill and an old problem. It makes the learning doubly difficult. The trick is to take responsibility for teaching yourself without relying completely on another person. Use your teacher to answer questions, and don't hesitate to ask those questions until you understand what you're being taught. Try things, even if stumbling is a very real possibility. Learn how to laugh at yourself.

Things that are tricky are explained in books and study guides that are always available to you. One of the things that makes *Fortune 500* companies dynamic, powerful, and successful is that they are constantly infused with new people and new ideas. People are hired from diverse professional and educational backgrounds and with wide-ranging (often unrelated) areas of expertise. The experience and information they bring with them are eclipsed by their ability to combine and recombine them into new and fascinating ideas. These environments are supercharged to create synergy, meaning that the end result of their efforts is more than the sum of the parts. One plus one equals three. (These corporations aren't *Fortune 500* companies by accident!)

When an organization such as emergency services limits the infusion of people and ideas, it fosters a very different environment: one of predictable outcome. This isn't a bad thing. In fact, predictability is vital when you're dealing with chaos and disaster day after day. But the point is that, when you use the materials the department provides for you, you learn what the department wants you to know. You'll mistakenly think that the keys to the universe are located between the covers of your departmental handbooks. You'll never consider the possibility of seeking out and bringing in other seemingly unrelated resources and adding them to your base of knowledge. Consequently, it's unlikely that you'll ever experience a synergetic moment, where something you've been taught suddenly combines with something you already knew and thereby creates magic. You have to be smart enough to realize that the world is vast and the possibilities and potentials are endless. Don't let the organization limit you and don't limit yourself.

Your job is unique in the workforce in that it provides blocks of downtime. Instead of watching TV between calls, you can study or practice skills at work. Unlike ambitious employees in the private sector, you won't have to put in a lot of personal time to get ahead. (This is especially useful if you're a volunteer and your time is limited by a regular job.)

No question about it. One of the real advantages of working in emergency services is that your hours are tightly controlled. Administration and unions carefully guard your time and energy so that you can be at your very best when you're on duty. No one wants you on an emergency call if you're too tired to make great decisions and withstand the enormous physical demands that are placed on you. The whole schedule is engineered to give you ample rest so that you'll replenish your physical, mental, and emotional stores between calls. Then, when the alarm sounds, you have 110 percent to give to the job. It takes that. The built-in downtime at work gives you ample opportunities for study and skill development. The problem is that, when you confine all of your development to your work environment, you tend to mistake it for professional development. That's okay if you're training to advance to a higher level of your present job or you aspire to be a manager or a supervisor. Training for work at work is entirely appropriate. But leadership development is both professional *and* personal. In fact, it's mostly personal. So, it's important that you carry that quest for development out the door and into your life.

In addition to having easy access to a clear promotion track, you have the benefit of being familiar with the facilities, equipment, organization, and people who work there. Admit it. You've been with your company so long that you've settled in. Like all human beings, once you're familiar with something, you tend to nestle down and get comfortable. You'll overlook flaws in the system if you can see them at all. Another very human foible is that we dislike change. Even you. Because you accept the familiar and resist change, you'll be more comfortable if you can maintain the status quo. There might be a million better ways of doing things, but too bad. If you were to come in from the outside, you wouldn't have this complacency. Since everything would be unfamiliar, nothing would be sacred. And disliking change would be beside the point, if not downright redundant. After all, you just changed jobs! Best of all, you would be bringing different experience and fresh perspective to a stale situation. You could really fine-tune the program. How many times has someone asked you why you do something and you've replied,

"Because that's the way we've always done it"? When you change positions within your own organization, you'll be tempted to think, "If it ain't broke, don't fix it." But things don't have to be broken for there to be room for improvement. You'll be surprised what you'll see when you're willing to abandon the comfort of familiarity and decide that change won't be so bad. Leadership requires that you be able to see the whole picture. You have to find a way to step back and view the organization from a vantage point far loftier and remote than the cozy little knoll you used to occupy.

The administration knows you. They are the people who will be considering you for promotion. They've seen your work and know what you can do. One of the most fascinating puzzles of corporate psychology is the mystique of the consultant. This is a total stranger who walks into a company and is given the benefit of complete credibility without having to produce the first result. In fact, the relationship between the organization and the consultant works well because it is based on the assumption that this total stranger knows more and is able to do more than any full-time employee in the whole company. A friend of mine who works as a consultant in Atlanta says that it's baffling even to her. After years of consulting, her theory is: "The companies don't know what I know. And they surely *don't* know what I don't know. They only *hope* that I know more than they do." I'm giving you this lesson in consulting to illustrate the power of hope. If you were to come to the workplace as an unknown quantity, people would have little sense of the limits of your knowledge and ability. You would have no baggage and no track record of failure. They would respond with hope. Not only would they give you the benefit of any doubt, they would also automatically assume that you had an untapped wealth of knowledge and ability. However, when you climb the ladder within your own organization, everyone knows you. Your track record is an open book. They know what you know. Worse, they know what you don't know. You'll have a lot to overcome and a lot of proving to do.

When you "grow up" in an organization, people tend to forget how you've grown. Negative images, impressions, and memories stick with everyone for a long time—even longer and more vividly than the positive ones. The administrative people might still see you as the wet-behind-the-ears rookie you once were. No matter how far you've progressed in your personal and professional development, there will be a lingering memory of you "before." Sometimes it's hard for a supervisor to overcome that.

Additionally, in emergency services there's a real division between "us" and "them"—employees and administration. Both sides do things that foster this sense of partition and keep psychological wedges driven between the two. Of course, everyone knows that we are all really on the same side, but our collective tendency is to make distinctions between the two. When you aspire to promotion from the employee level, you are reaching toward the administrative level. You—one of "us"—are asking to become one of "them." Frankly, administration is a closed society that has shut you out for a long time. Turnabout is fair play. You've done the same thing to them. But now you're knocking on their door and asking to be let in. For someone in administration to make the psychological adjustment necessary to open that door, thinking and orientation have to be seriously adjusted. People in administration have to see in you something that will more closely align you with "them" than with "us." There has to be some spark, some ... hope.

Your coworkers know what you know and who you are. They know what to expect. The toughest transitions you'll make in your career are when you break ranks with your brothers and sisters to pursue your climb up the organization's ladder. With every promotion, you leave "us" behind and move ever closer to "them," the brass. These transitions are made even more difficult by the reactions of your buddies. You'll feel like a turncoat anyway. They'll make you feel worse. Their reactions will start when you announce your intentions or prepare to apply. They'll end ... maybe never. Here are some common reactions:

"You got the job I should have had." This sentiment surfaces when more than one person is in contention for only a single position. When career advancement is viewed as a competition, it's natural to think in terms of winning and losing. You won. Your competitors lost. But career advancement isn't a contest. The person who gets the job doesn't beat anyone out of it. Although everyone knows this on an intellectual level, the reality is small consolation to those who didn't get the job you were offered. They will feel disappointed and humiliated by their failure to outperform you. Because it's too hard

to admit that maybe they weren't as qualified as you were, they'll look for ways to justify your promotion that include *everything* except that you were more qualified.

"*You're doing something I should have done.*" Some people turn their attention immediately to an intense examination of their own performances and qualifications. They vow that next time they'll do better and decide to use you as the template for success. They ask, "What exactly did you *do* to get this promotion and how can I do the same the next time?" This would be good except that they'll be comparing and contrasting themselves with you, point by point. Every mistake you ever made will come under microscopic scrutiny. Every great thing you ever did will be reframed as "sucking up." Once they've finished running you through a meat grinder, they'll arrive at some hideous conclusions about their own inadequacies. To correct those inadequacies requires emulating you. Because they're angry at you, it's a sickening thought.

"*You think you're too good for us.*" Emergency services engenders the illusion that you and your coworkers are siblings—brothers and sisters. You're all equals in the family with Mom and Dad way above you, running the company. When you get promoted, there is a pervasive feeling among your siblings that you betrayed the silent deal you all made to be equal. Let me explain it in terms of your own childhood.

When you were little kids and your parents went out for the evening, they appointed your big brother to babysit all the rest of you. Instantly you resented his power and vowed to do everything you could think of to undermine his authority and let him know that you didn't respect his new position. Your poor brother did nothing that was authoritative. He simply retreated as usual to his bedroom to do his homework without a word to you. It didn't matter. You were seething. That big uppity big shot had to be put back into his place. Hey, he wasn't the boss of you.

The same thing happens today when a "sibling" in the department is given authority. The rest of the "kids" bristle with resentment. There's an instant leap to assume that the newly promoted coworker is an uppity big shot who needs to be brought down a hitch or two. If you are that uppity big shot, you'll likely experience passive-aggressive behavior (the grown-up version of a little kid's vow to undermine your authority and demonstrate a lack of respect). Passive-aggressive behavior is sneaky because it isn't open hostility. You'll just notice subtle little ways of stonewalling you to make things hard for you. The perpetrators don't actually do anything wrong. They just don't do anything. They don't commit an act of treason. They just omit a helping hand. It can be confusing and maddening.

Another aspect of your seeking a promotion and leaving your "siblings" is that, when you leave them, you send a loud, clear message that their level isn't good enough for you anymore. They feel rejected. They think that you're looking down on them and judging their decision to remain on that level as lacking ambition. Either that, or you're judging their inability to rise within the organization as a reflection of their incompetence. You're going to have to do a lot of reassuring with words and actions to get them to relax and realize that your move has nothing to do with them.

"You did something underhanded to get that promotion." It's hard for the people who didn't get your job to admit that you were more qualified and that they failed to perform to your level. It's much easier to consider the possibility that you did something sneaky and underhanded to get that promotion. Actually, this is only an attempt to keep your sibling deal—that you're all equals. In bringing you down a notch, they keep you on their level. Once again, you are equals—except that you're a sly dog who did something (they're not sure what) to get that job. In time, they'll settle down and come to their senses. Until then, you have to conduct yourself in a manner that reminds them that you're still the same forthright person you always were.

"We'll never be able to trust you again." When you work, train, play, eat, sleep, and shower with people, you get to know them pretty well. For as long as you've been together, you've all enjoyed a special camaraderie. But that's over now. Once you're promoted, your relationship with them will make a subtle shift, and friendships as you all knew it will change. Suddenly you have more power, prestige, information, and authority than they do. You're no longer equals in the organization. Although I know of a few cases where higher-ranking people have been able to maintain friendship with lower-ranking ones, experience tells me that it's pretty rare. Even in these mature and cemented friendships, there can come a moment

when one has to pull rank on the other. Within seconds, the easy give-and-take dynamics of friendship are overruled by the strict and necessary hierarchy of the workplace. I assure you that this isn't easy for either friend, especially the lower-ranking one.

The biggest problem is that, when you leave one camp and enter another, you're carrying proprietary information. Coworkers tell secrets. They share quiet opinions. They cover up mistakes. They plot, plan, consort, and conspire. They gripe and complain. They gossip. All of this clandestine communication is the private domain of coworkers and should *never* make its way up the ladder to administration. When you move up that ladder, you carry their secrets with you. Like an enemy spy, you take information where it was never intended to be heard. You're now in a perfect position for betraying confidences and using private information against buddies. Your coworkers are greatly concerned about how you will use that information to exert power and control.

Without question, one of the great joys of camaraderie is this sharing of secrets. Get used to the harsh reality that, once you're promoted, you're out of the loop. No more secret telling for you. It's possible that you'll still be privy to small things from time to time, but you will never again be on the inside of the old gang. Cheer up. You're now part of a new group of people who also share secrets—different secrets to be sure, but secrets all the same.

Respect the secrets you brought with you. Keep your mouth closed. Sooner or later, your buddies will observe an incident where it'll be easy for you to unveil a confidence and use it as a weapon. When you don't, your buddies will realize that you're to be trusted and will relax.

Firm Footing on the Slippery Steps Up the Ladder of Success

This is your career. You are in complete control of it. Nothing and no one can stop you. If you aspire to excellence (and you do), you're going to climb the ladder of success. You need to know that the climb will never be easy. If it were, anyone could scramble right up. I've outlined many of the stumbling blocks that will be part and parcel of your professional adventure. Rather than being discouraged, you should regard the outline as a glimpse into the dark side of rising in the ranks. Now you are aware of the problems before they arise and can prepare yourself to meet the challenges they present.

Being aware of problems and heading them off at the pass are effective in making promotion easier, but there's more you can do to gain a firm footing.

Find a mentor. Identify a senior person within the organization who's willing to take you under his wing and guide you. You want someone who's been there so that you can benefit from his experience. This new relationship between the two of you doesn't have to be formal. In fact, often the relationship simply evolves naturally between people when one person reaches out and another person takes hold. The more experienced person is the mentor. The relationship is more than that of student and instructor. An instructor teaches you *how* to do something. A mentor helps you understand *why* you're doing it. A mentor allows you to sharpen your skills while you deepen your understanding, and opens your world just a little wider than you could on your own.

Look to the future. Success is no accident. It's carefully laid out in a step-by-step plan. Human resources experts tell us that successful people look to the future and know how they're going to get there. They have personal mission statements that define their purposes in life, and consequently everything they do is in sync with their missions. No move is haphazard. No energy is wasted. They have five-year plans, ten-year plans, and lifetime plans—all engineered to support clear goals that result from their mission statements. To test the path between today and tomorrow, they create future case scenarios. When they can "see" the outcome, they can figure out how to get there methodically. One technique they use is to think and speak of the future as if it has already happened. To be a laser-focused person, it's helpful to have a mission statement and a chronological plan to fulfill that mission.

Write your mission statement. Developing your personal mission statement is a good way to clarify your purpose in life. Experts advise that it should be short—no more than a sentence—and simple. It should be broad enough to cover both your personal and professional lives. Before you construct the sentence, you must decide how you're going to accomplish your life's work. Express it in action words—verbs. Then determine what you're going to devote your energy to. Express this as your cause—a noun. Finally, name those who will benefit or be affected by your taking action toward your cause. Express this as a noun. A mission statement is constructed like this:

"My mission is to _____ (action expressed in verbs) _____ (your cause, a noun) to, with, or for _____(whom your mission will serve).

Here are some examples:

"My mission is to promote safety with all of the people I meet."
"My mission is to inspire, recognize, and honor the highest ideals of leadership in myself and others."
"My mission is to create a safe, fire-free, and crime-free environment for myself, my family, and my community."

Mission statements are as individual as the people who create them, as yours will be.

Making your plan. Once you have a mission statement, you can plan your future. Take a few minutes and make a chronological list, making certain that each step on your list is consistent with your mission.

The position I want in five years is_____.
The position I want in ten years is_____.
The position I ultimately want is_____.

Your list could be much longer with shorter intervals between the steps, but now that you have the list, construct a plan to move from one step to the other until you've reached the ultimate position. Or, start with the ultimate position and go backward. Remember to state the future as if it has already happened. You could say:

"I am on the faculty of the National Fire Academy.

"So, ten years before that, I need to be chief of my department and the president of the International Association of Fire Chiefs and hold a master's degree from a major university. Also, I need to have a reputation as a good teacher, so I need to have experience with workshops.

"So, five years before that, I need to be a captain, hold an office with the IAFC, be enrolled in graduate school, and volunteer to speak at workshops.

"So, *today* I need to study for my lieutenant's exam, work on a committee with the IAFC, enroll in the local college to finish my bachelor's degree, and join Toastmasters to learn to speak in front of groups."

You get the idea. Planning your future is a methodical, logical, step-by-step process that keeps you focused on moving forward, keeping all of the impediments out of your line of sight.

Partner with key players. If you want to soar with eagles, you have to leave the turkeys on the ground. Aligning yourself with powerful people is a good way to sneak a peek at what it takes to get where they are. If you're astute, you'll pick up pointers on behaviors and practices that separate the leaders from the followers. They'll teach you to set your sights high and serve as living proof to you that, if they achieved success, so can you. Success rubs off. You'll soon find yourself emulating the key players you're studying. Friends in high places can be useful when you're looking for a mentor. Mentors come from the *upper* echelons, not from the lower levels.

Finally, if key players already know you, they can put in a good word for you when you're being considered for promotion. The more familiar they are with you, the less you'll have to overcome when you're on the hot seat in interviews.

The View Gets Better
With Every Step Up

Making the decision that you're aiming for the top is easy. Getting there is more difficult, but it's well worth the effort. The higher in rank you go, the better able you are to serve people. That is, after all, why you're in emergency services.

PERSONAL STUDY EXERCISES

1. Design your mission statement.

2. Write your ultimate goal in a sentence as if it has already happened. Write a step-by-step plan, broken into five-year increments, to get you there.

3. Make a list of accessible people in the department who are older, wiser, and more experienced than you are. Identify one whom you would like to have as your mentor. Develop strategies for moving closer to that person to enter into a mentor relationship.

CHAPTER 4

Change Is the Only Constant in Life

"The game [of chess] is so full of events, there is such a variety of turns in it, the fortune of it is so subject to sudden vicissitudes, and one so frequently, after contemplation, discovers the means of extricating one's self from a supposed insurmountable difficulty, that one is encouraged to continue to contest the last ...."

—Ben Franklin

Nothing ever stays the same. Just when you have everything figured out, something happens to shatter your theories. Just when you have everything where you want it, something moves. Just when you think you know someone, he does something so totally unexpected that you realize that you are essentially strangers to each other. Just when you have a medical emergency under control, another symptom surfaces. Just when you have one fire extinguished, another one flares up. Constant change is one of the immutable laws of the universe and so basic to the nature of life itself that it is ironic that we, as human beings, are so resistant. Someone should have sat us down at the beginning and whispered, "Want to know the secret of all things? I'll give you a hint. Think flux."

Changing Yourself

Someone defined insanity as "Doing the same things over and over again and expecting a different outcome each time." If things are going to be different in your life, something has to change. Doing what you've been doing is going to get you what you've been getting, but you no longer want that. You are poised to step into leadership. You have to do things differently now. You might even have to *be* different. For most people, change can be a daunting prospect. In fact, I'll tell you a secret. You aren't going to have a lot of competition in your quest for leadership because most people are just too afraid of change to take the risks you're willing to take. Winners do all the things that other people aren't willing to tackle. Even if you, yourself, have had a queasy moment—a tremor of uncertainty—I'm going to demystify personal change for you so that you will be comfortable and confident as you move into the future that you create for yourself.

I want to laugh whenever I hear someone imply that he is firmly cast in stone and that change is out of the question. The trigger phrases are, "I always ..." or "I never ..." or "I can't ...." The truth is, *you can change.* It doesn't matter how resistant you are to the idea of change. Frankly, you are really, really good at it. You've been doing it since the day you were conceived. You started out as a couple of cells, and look at you now! Science teaches us that we, as human beings, are miracles of transformation and morphing. Researchers report that we continuously regenerate most of the cells in our bodies throughout our lifetimes and completely regenerate our skin approximately every three weeks! DNA encoding makes sure that the new you looks pretty much like the old you, but your cells are being replaced all the time. When you get scraped, you heal. Dead skin sloughs off and reveals bright, new skin that's forming underneath. Your hair falls out and then regrows. Fingernails grow no matter how often you file them. You're renewing all the time. Trust me. Trust the evidence. You're good at change.

I point out that you're good at physical change because I want to obliterate any reluctance or excuses about your ability to change. Although I'll admit that nearly all of the credit for our physical bodies goes to Mother Nature, within the process of physical regeneration, we do exert a measure of control. For example, you're as fat or as thin as you've decided to be. You've literally sculpted yourself through diet and exercise (or lack thereof). Your hair is the color, length, and style you have decided is most flattering to you. The same is true of all people. The packages you see when you look at other people are the packages they want you to see—the packages they think portray them. They use such tools as makeup, contact lenses, glasses, cosmetic dentistry, plastic surgery, jewelry, clothing, shoes, adornments, facial hair, tattoos, foundation garments, body language, and facial expressions to alter their appearances. Conversely, when they look at you, they see the package that you engineer and decide is best for them to see. *You* engineer your package. *You* change your appearance to suit the image of yourself that you think is best.

As impressive as control over the physical body may be, the real power is in the mind of the human being. The mind is the one place where possibilities and potentials are limitless; where change—albeit imaginary—is instantaneous. *Thought* is the basic building block of change. In thought, you can envision your future, design your change, plan your strategy, determine possible outcomes, correct mistakes before they happen, and make that ultimate decision to move. It all happens in imagination before it takes place in reality. You have full control. Napoleon Hill wrote, "What the mind of man can conceive and believe, the mind of man can achieve."

So, How Do You Change?

Personal change is really quite simple. It happens when one aspect of your life evolves into something else. It isn't the explosive intrusion of a totally new you. You don't fall asleep one night as one person and wake up another, unless you're starring in a gothic horror movie and the script involves a vial of something green and a stunt double who looks nothing like you. The real-life process of change is gradual. Once you understand that to change yourself is to evolve yourself, then you can look on change as a series of controlled, creative, disciplined events.

Before you run off to change yourself, there are a few ground rules. From the outset, I caution you to be realistic about your plans. Plan to change only those things you can change. Forget aspiring to be a foot taller or grow an extra thumb, and concentrate on aspects of your life that are malleable. Likely, you'll know the differences between aspirations that are truly attainable and those that are strictly pie in the sky. Be careful, however, to give careful consideration to that goal that might, at first glance, seem unattainable. Sometimes, with a little creative thinking, a pie in the sky can be a piece of cake. Cutting yourself short is a habit developed by a lifetime of predictable outcomes from doing things the "old way."

Remember what I told you earlier, that doing what you've been doing is going to get you what you've been getting. If you're going to change, your possibilities will, too.

1. *Understand exactly who you are and what your circumstances are.* The first step in evolving yourself is to understand exactly who you are and what your circumstances are. Because evolving is changing something already in existence, you have to figure out what that is. Sit down and take a hard, honest look at yourself and your circumstances, particularly those things that are not working for you. If you're like most of us, at first you'll zero in on something huge. You might identify a bad work habit you have or a perceived flaw in your personality, such as a hot temper. It's easy to spot the big problems in your life because they come into focus most easily. They're the most obvious. Once they have your attention, they become the most uncomfortable. Having found something huge, you might be tempted to leap in to make broad, sweeping changes to turn that discomfort around. Slow down. There's no easier way to become overwhelmed and defeated before you begin than to try to change something you're not clear about. From the start, be certain that the thing you want to change is specific and that you understand it thoroughly. Often you'll find that even the largest problem is really a composite of several smaller ones. You'd be doomed to failure if you've examined your life and circumstances and concluded that "I'm not a good person. I need to change to become better." This would be too general a change to which to aspire. This assessment, made more specific and clear, might be a general reflection of your need to correct three things you were able to pinpoint—things that keep you from feeling that you're the best you could be. You notice that you can't hold up your end of a conversation when it turns to current events, you aren't as physically fit as you would like to be, and you think you could offer a lot to your community if you would only make the time. Change is more easily managed when you can break your uneasy circumstances into smaller components that can be examined and evolved individually. When you examine the things that need changing one at a time, ways to change emerge one at a time.

2. *Take responsibility for who you are and how you've been responding to*

your circumstances. Only when you understand that you are responsible do you have the power to change things. Frankly, powerless people are stuck. The assumption of responsibility is tricky, because it's really tough to admit that your life—both good and bad—is of your own making. You created it. You chose it. Great stuff is your triumph. Bad stuff is your fault. Even when your circumstances are undeniably out of your control, you still choose your consequent reaction and action. I know that you're standing up now, pointing your finger at this page, and shouting, "Yeah, but .... Yeah, but .... Yeah, but ...." Sorry, I have to take a hard line here. It wouldn't be honest of me to cut you any slack. You have to understand that you can change *nothing* if you have no power, and the only way to have power is to *know* that you were and *are* always in control. A few years ago, when I had that terrible accident at the Daytona International Speedway, my body was just too broken to be rebuilt to meet the rigorous physical standards of the fire-rescue service. When I realized that the career I loved with all my heart was over, it was a terrible moment for me. The accident had been out of my control. It had been just that—an *accident.* But how I reacted to the new circumstance and how I took action were fully in my control. Here is the process I used to change—to *evolve*— myself within that corridor of my life.

A. The accident happens. Although I admit that I put myself in the "wrong place at the wrong time," I did not cause the accident. It's a circumstance out of my control.

B. To the best of my ability, I engineer a stunning rehabilitation, but, as time passes, I am aware that my body is too damaged to return it to its former strength and function.

C. After disappointing testing, I realize that I can no longer meet the physical requirements of firefighting and emergency medical services.

D. I understand and support the need for physical standards that protect the well-being of my colleagues and the people we serve. I choose to continue to support those standards. I am responsible for my decision to withdraw from active firefighting and emergency medical services.

E. I have always been in charge of my professional life. I choose to continue to be in charge of my professional life.

F. I am well aware of my strengths and weaknesses, personally and professionally. I use this knowledge to adapt my love of firefighting and emergency medical services to something that accommodates my new strengths and weaknesses.

G. I change my profession from fire-rescue to *teacher.*

H. I become a consultant, author, and professional speaker.

Please note that I acknowledged responsibility and asserted control everywhere that I was able. The outcome might have been radically different if I had succumbed to being a victim of the accident and later a victim of the bureaucracy that set standards I couldn't meet. Action and evolution were possible for me only because I knew I was in charge—not of the circumstances, but of *me.* Because I was in charge, I could generate options and make choices for change. I was able to transform one profession into another.

3. *Figure out what you want.* Generating options brings me to the third step in personal change: Figure out what you want. You have to be able to state your desired outcome in clear, unwavering terms. Having stated this clearly defined goal not only gives you a direction toward which you take action, it also lets you know when you've achieved it. In setting your goal, you also have to set a time line. If you think "someday," then your goal looks suspiciously like a dream. "Someday" gives you too much latitude to wander off your mission.

4. *Plan your change.* When you set a goal to change something and put it on a hard deadline, then you're ready for this fourth step. This is a process of possibility thinking. Do this exercise with a pad and pen. It's time for a little time travel. Envision yourself with the change already in place and get clear about when it finally happened. Let's say that you have decided to be 15 pounds leaner in one year. Picture yourself one year from today and 15 pounds leaner. Now, back up by one month. What were you doing during that month that brought about your desired result? Likely, you were working out at the gym (just as you had for the past 11 months) and eating healthy food, and you only had one pound left to lose.

Back up one more month. What were you doing during the 10th month that brought you—on target—to the 11th month's outcome? Keep backing up—month by month, week by week, day by day—until you are at tomorrow. Now you know precisely how to start and at what pace you have to progress in your efforts to lose 15 pounds in one year. Part of the problem in making change is that the process can seem formidable and overwhelming. When you break change down into small steps and plan systematic action to get you from one step to the next, then change doesn't seem like such a big deal. You can be confident that you're in complete control over the process. Clearly, change is merely evolution.

5. *Take action.* Change begins to happen when you move on it. Until then, it's just one of your good ideas. I have a friend who once offered to share with me the secret to unlocking personal potential and power for change. I eagerly listened, prepared to take notes and swear mystical oaths of silence. She looked me straight in the eye, lowered her voice, and said, "Go clean out a drawer." I drew back in disbelief, certain that I had either misunderstood her or had been taken in by her warped sense of humor. She repeated the secret, "Go clean out a drawer." I laughed right out loud. She repeated it again and added seriously, "Do it, Mike." I thought she was insane, but I had a drawer that had needed cleaning for a long time, so when I went off duty, I cleaned it out. There was no great moment of truth, but it felt really good. When I returned to the station, I reported in to my friend. I said, "OK, I cleaned out the drawer. So now what?" She asked me to tell her how it felt to tackle a task that had been hanging over me for so long. As I told her about the experience, I realized that, although I hadn't thought about the cluttered drawer, it had bothered me. Not much. Just a little. When I finally cleaned it out, the task proved not to be difficult and took only a few minutes. The reward of the tidy drawer was almost insignificant when I compared it with my contentment for getting that task off my to-do list. In fact, I had to admit that cleaning the drawer had given me a heady feeling. I started to think that, if it only took ten minutes to get that problem out of my life, then I could clean out another drawer and another. It was a small leap into thinking that I could do anything. My friend smiled knowingly. The secret key to

unlocking personal potential and power is to take action. Her point was well made. Often the anticipation of the undone task or the needed change is far worse than the actual doing. Incomplete tasks and unresolved issues sap us of our strength and power. It's best to leap in and do something—to do anything that will move us in the direction of our goals.

Make Those Changes One at a Time

Now that you know how easy and manageable change can be, you might be tempted to make a huge list of things you would like to change. Rein in your enthusiasm just a little. It's best to keep it simple and tackle those changes one at a time. Going back to our "better person" example, rather than to resolve to "be a better person," it would be better to say, "I would be a better person if I read more newspapers and magazines, went to the gym on a regular basis, and volunteered at a community assistance program." Please note that, even if you observe and examine three different aspects of your life that need changing, you will only be successful at making those changes if you tackle one change at a time. We are creatures of habit and easily overwhelmed by too much change too fast. It's better to slow down and make sure you're getting it right.

If you're like most people, you'll have the greatest success when you work to change one thing at a time. Changing one thing focuses your entire attention and increases your chances of getting it right. I assure you that nothing begets success like success. Every positive change you make gives you more power and command of the process and makes every subsequent change more manageable. I had a friend who announced that he had decided to become a champion bodybuilder. Without insulting my friend, I have to tell you that this was a huge undertaking for a previously sedentary man (and I mean "sedentary" in the least flattering way!). In spite of our best (and unsolicited) advice, my buddy set his goal and made a list that included: find a gym, join the gym, hire a trainer, set a schedule into his calendar, purchase a workout log, hire a nutritionist, meet with the nutritionist, set up appointments, organize a new diet, purchase an eating log, identify and purchase nutritional supplements, clean out his refrigerator, buy new groceries, buy a new cookbook, learn to cook healthy food, purchase workout clothing and shoes, purchase an industrial-sized gym bag, lay in his training regimen, get to the gym once a day for an hour, and on and on. By the time he had it all organized, he was exhausted. His financial resources were stretched to the limit. His friends and family chafed at the "new and improved" life he preached (that insultingly excluded them). It didn't take long for him to discover that some of his master plan worked and some of it didn't, but because he had locked all of it into place at one time, he had very little room for adjustment. His work started to slip. His enthusiasm fizzled. Worse, three weeks into the project, he had a moment of truth: that he wasn't a champion bodybuilder. He was the only one surprised. He was, in fact, a discouraged, sore, starving man with too much spandex in his closet. Predictably, he quit. (As a side note, I will tell you that we welcomed him back into the fold of normal people and celebrated his return at a local pizza parlor, where bodies are built with pepperoni.)

The lesson in all of this is that my friend might be a champion bodybuilder today had he made the changes one at a time, fine-tuning each as he progressed. Or, he might have adjusted his plan. He might have discovered that he merely liked being physically fit. He might have decided that being a champion wasn't necessary to feeling great. Now we'll never know. My friend, enthusiastic and human, defied the ground rules of change: Be realistic and change one thing at a time.

Change Can Be (Temporarily) Dangerous

I'm going to warn you now. While you're in the process of change, you're going to be vulnerable. It's like being a trapeze artist: As you swing above the ground without a net, there's a breathless moment when you let go of one trapeze, turn, and reach out into the air to take hold of another trapeze. Change is like that. There's a breathless, heart-stopping moment when you let go of one idea and reach out for another. In that moment, you hold on to nothing. No old idea. No new idea. Just a moment in the air without a net. I live in Florida, where sea stories are popular, so I'll tell one about change and the Florida lobster. The Florida lobster's life is interesting. He grows to be quite large, but his shell doesn't grow along with him. In fact, it doesn't grow at all. Therefore, it's necessary at intervals for the lobster to shed his old shell so he can grow a new one. In that interim between the old and new shells, he's soft and defenseless—the target of every hungry predator on the reef. The lobster's life is in grave danger, but he sheds anyway because his old shell just doesn't fit anymore and he needs to grow. Changing will be the same for you. To grow and change, you have to be vulnerable. Every predator in your life will try to attack you. Those who perceive change as an indicator that you're wavering in your thinking and see your transformation as a sure sign of weakness will use it as an opportunity to strike. Other people will not be supportive, and worse, will try to make you feel silly. Be patient and understanding. These new opponents might be threatened by your taking control of your life. Your successful efforts might make them feel guilty about all of the things they want to change but can't figure out how. They might be afraid that you'll change so much that you'll no longer find them interesting. Remember, if you can hang in there, you'll get your shell back. You'll toughen up. Best of all, you'll have grown.

Responding to Change That Happens Around You

The fire-rescue profession exists because of the need to manage change—specifically, emergencies. The word "emergency" itself means "the emergence of a situation." It is further defined as sudden, unexpected, and demanding immediate action. Of course, the ability to respond with immediate action is your personal and professional stock in trade. As a firefighter-EMT, you're trained to restore order, or at least mitigate bad situations.

1. *Get as much experience and exposure as you can.* The deeper your bag of tricks—that is, the more experience you have—the better able you are to handle an emergency or any other change that happens around you. There's a lot to be said for the quiet confidence of "been there, done that." My advice is to get out there and experience as much as you can. Of course, time will be a great teacher. The longer you live and the more fully you participate in your life, the more exposure you'll have to situations and people from whom you can learn. Working in emergency services gives you a sort of crash course

in life. You'll see, hear, and experience more, and more intensely, than most people ever will. It's a good thing, too. You need that information to draw on in your work, because, as we say in the fire station, just when you think you've seen it all, you ain't seen nothing yet.

2. *Read and study.* If you don't have the time to experience everything (and you don't), read about it instead. Reading allows you to benefit from the experience of others. In fact, often when an author writes about resolving a situation, he will expound on it, giving you great insight into the source of the solution. And information that is seemingly irrelevant at the time can suddenly surface later as useful. I can't tell you how many times I've asked, "How did you know how to do that?" and had the person reply, "I don't know. I guess I read it somewhere." I once complimented a friend of mine on her ability to handle a particularly difficult employee and asked where she had learned such sophisticated management skills. She said simply, "Puppy training manual. Chapter Four. I'm using the simple command-and-reward system on him." (By the way, she assures me that she has never swatted the guy with a rolled-up newspaper!) The point is that the puppy training manual is, at first glance, unrelated to her workplace, but my friend is nimble in her thinking and able to make associations of useful information when she needs them. Additionally, reading is an activity that you can do privately, on your own schedule, in bits and pieces. It doesn't take a huge commitment from a busy person.

3. *Listen.* Take the time to listen to as many people as you can. When you find a person who's found a solution for a difficult problem, ask for details. The value of the answer will be in the process used, not the outcome. Pack your bag of tricks with other people's experience.

4. *Be willing to be wrong.* One of the best ways to be light on your feet when you're faced with a situation in flux is to be willing to be wrong. It is when you get stubborn and dig in that you lose your ability to examine another point of view. When I first started as a young firefighter, I was sometimes hesitant and tentative in my approach to my work. I was concerned that, if I made a mistake, the consequences would be earth-shattering in ways that only a blundering, stumbling rookie can shatter the earth. (Not to mention that I didn't

want to embarrass myself.) I worked for a fellow who observed my nearly imperceptible reluctance to leap into certain situations. One day he took me aside and said, "Mike, the only person who doesn't make a mistake is the person who doesn't do anything at all. Trust your training and common sense. Do something. If it's wrong, we'll deal with it." His wise words have served me well in my career.

5. *Play out the possibilities.* When you're in a situation that is slip-sliding, play "What If I Do and What If I Don't?" Nothing facilitates flexible thinking more than to quickly think around the corners of the situation. Play out all the possibilities. Take a rapid stand or make a rapid decision, and then consider all the possible outcomes of the action you would take. Now, switch positions. Take another stand. Make another decision. Anticipate all the possibilities. Do this until one stand or decision yields the best potential for outcome. Then move. All of this should take no more than a split second. Being a thoughtful, contemplative person is good, but not always in emergency situations. You have to be fast and decisive. The trick is to take action, not merely *react* to situations. Taking action means that you've consciously chosen which move to make. Conscious choice is preceded by thought. Of course, the more experienced you are, the more quickly you can scan your mental databases for information, but don't let lack of experience stop you. You'll make the best decision, based on the best information you have at hand. Learn to trust yourself and be a person who can think on his feet and then act.

6. *Learn to fail and practice it.* One of the successful strategies for dealing with change is to learn how to fail and practice it. Let me explain that. Author Pearl S. Buck said, "Every great mistake has a halfway moment, a split-second when it can be recalled and perhaps remedied." But you cannot identify that halfway moment if you haven't crossed it at some point. In firefighting and emergency services, we're trained to keep a given situation from reaching the "halfway moment." In doing so, however, we seldom (if ever) encounter opportunities for exercising our judgment in "off-the-chart" crises. Situations change in emergency services. If you're a person who stands in the midst of chaos and can't accept that things have taken a turn for the worse, you'll die. If you can't admit that you've failed and

you need to adjust your plan, you'll die. If you're too blind to recognize that halfway moment and pass it without thinking, you'll die. And worse, others will die with you. Practicing to fail is critical to survival. It's well known that reactions during crises are not creative; they are either instinctive or the result of overtraining—doing something over and over and over until it becomes second nature. In training, you need to construct and practice drills that allow your crew to experience that feeling of failure—when all of you know that you're not going to win this particular battle but that you are all going to live to tell the tale. Sometimes, losing means you've won. Big time.

The best way for me to illustrate the triumphs and failures of dealing with change is through the story of Mann Gulch. On August 4, 1949, a small forest wildfire broke out in the Helena National Forest. When it was over, 13 firefighters were dead. Later, fire examiners would speculate that it was probably caused by a common lightning strike. The wildfire might have had an ordinary cause, but its consequences were anything but ordinary. The fire had escalated into fury during the night. The next day was windy and hot—the thermometer read 97°F, and the fire danger rating was 74 out of a possible 100. At this point, 15 trained firefighters—smoke jumpers—were dispatched into the area to bring the blaze under control. Even they underestimated the blaze, calling it a "10 o'clock fire," meaning they felt confident that they would have it under control by 10 o'clock. They were mistaken. Historians and poets now call the Mann Gulch fire "a race the firefighters couldn't win."

There was trouble from the beginning in a mind-numbing litany of mistakes, misinformation, and misconceptions that collectively led to disaster. The air above the drop site was so turbulent that the crew was forced to ascend from the usual 1,200 feet to 2,000 feet before they jumped. One of the men became so airsick that he took off his parachute, withdrew from the mission, returned to base, and resigned immediately. The radio's parachute failed to open and the radio shattered on impact with the ground. In spite of an ominous start, all of the jumpers landed safely in the forest. As if this were business as usual, they met with forest service ranger Jim Harrison, who had been fighting the fire alone on the mountain for four hours. The crew took time to eat supper. Then they gathered supplies and discussed tactics.

Under the leadership of foreman "Wag" Dodge and ranger Harrison, the crew moved into position. Dodge and Harrison had scouted the area together while the crew ate and were admittedly uneasy about the thick forest that surrounded them and the potential it held for feeding an out-of-control fire. Their vague worry turned to alarm when Dodge discovered that the fire had crossed the gulch just 200 yards ahead of them and was moving toward them. He shouted for the crew to turn around and head up the hill through tall grass toward the ridge above the fire. The fire was gaining on them with flames 30 feet high, moving more than 600 feet per minute. Dodge quickly reassessed the urgency of the situation and ordered the crew to drop their heavy tools and run. Then he lit a fire in front of them and shouted for them to follow him into the burned area and lie down. No one in the crew obeyed Dodge's new orders. Clearly, they thought he was insane. They all scrambled toward the ridge in an ill-fated attempt to outrun the fire. Only two made it through a crevice in the ridge. The rest of the crew—13 men—perished in the fire. It took less than 15 minutes. Dodge would rise from the safe haven of his ashes to the certain knowledge that his men were dead because they had not trusted him.

The U.S. Forest Service concluded that Dodge was blameless and acknowledged that the crew could have been saved if they had followed his orders and gone with him into his escape fire. Being cleared must have been small consolation to Dodge. His men were dead.

Every firefighter who examines the reports will notice two things: First, the smoke jumpers disobeyed their commander; and second, their bodies were recovered with their tools in hand or very nearby. In other words, they did not drop their heavy gear to outrun the fire. Even if we can understand reluctance to follow a command that seems illogical, it is nearly incomprehensible to us that a firefighter would rather die than leave a chainsaw behind. And yet it happened.

Behavioral experts have studied the Mann Gulch tragedy extensively and have offered several theories about the reasons these men might have had for disobeying orders and refusing to drop their tools and follow Dodge into his escape fire. But they all agree that a collective inability to manage change contributed to the tragedy.

First, the firefighters made an assessment that the fire was routine. When evidence to the contrary presented itself, they apparently stubbornly clung to their original assessment. There is an all-too-human tendency to explain away any information that doesn't match our thinking. If you saw your dog flying across the yard, you simply wouldn't accept it. It wouldn't matter that you were personally witnessing it. You would match this new turn of events against all that you believe—that dogs are ground-bound and can't fly. The second thing you would do is frantically search for a logical explanation. Practical joke by a friend who rigged your dog to a wire. Dog ran up an incline and leaped—it only looks like he's flying. You're hallucinating (bad tacos last night). You'll continue to scan your personal experience and knowledge for an explanation until you've proved to yourself that what you're seeing isn't true. Now, there's nothing wrong with being skeptical and practical, but a truly facile mind would at least consider the *possibility* that a talented dog can fly. In keeping an open mind and considering all of the evidence, you give yourself the opportunity to detect and react to changes. If the firefighters at Mann Gulch had been able to do this, they might have been able to more quickly and accurately assess the changing nature of the fire and make better decisions.

Second, the firefighters at Mann Gulch couldn't understand the concept of the escape fire that Wag Dodge built to shelter them from the raging inferno that threatened to overtake them. They had never seen one before and were unable to see the potential it held for saving them. Dodge was using fire in an innovative way, but his idea was too radical for the firefighters to accept it. Simply, the escape fire didn't fit into their knowledge or experience, and they were too panicked to give the idea time to sink in. Again, being able to use something in a new context requires changing one's mind, shifting one's thinking, suspending belief, and being creative. This rarely happens for the first time in a crisis situation when human beings react rather than create. In a crisis, instinct takes over. Thinking is set aside. The person moves. Of course, there are rare individuals like Wag Dodge who are able to step aside from a crisis, quell fear, and clear their heads to think. But most of us are incapable of this nearly superhuman ability unless we are practiced at being flexible thinkers who can engage the intellect in the face of contradictory evidence. These are the people who can deal with change and make change happen.

Finally, the firefighters at Mann Gulch were unable to accept failure. One of the nearly incomprehensible things they did was to cling to their heavy tools, even though dropping them might have allowed them to outrun the fire. Behavioral experts have theorized that firefighters are defined by their tools, just as warriors are defined by their weapons. Putting down their tools strips them of their identity. They are no longer firefighters, because they have nothing to fight with. And worse, to put down tools and run is to admit defeat—a concept that is completely alien and harshly unacceptable to people who are trained to win. There can be no clearer demonstration of how stubbornly human beings cling to old ideas that aren't working than to realize that they'd rather die than let go. Firefighters and emergency services personnel have a mindset that's particularly difficult to overcome. We have to win. Winning is the reason we exist. None of us responds to a call and says to the family, "OK, we're here. We'll save your home after we talk it over and decide that it's a good idea." No. Emergency response means that every member snaps into instantaneous battle mode when the call comes in. We race to the problem and fix it. Always. No one waffles. Because the situations are sometimes dangerous, we're required to do things that would cause a sane person to think twice. To do something truly dangerous requires a focused sense of mission and a certainty that the risk is worth the successful outcome. Our identities as firefighters or emergency services personnel limit or mitigate the catastrophic results of the emergency. To do that, you assess the situation, consider all of the possibilities, make decisions, take charge, and take action. Further, experience has taught you that, when everything looks good, you restrain the urge to get smug. You know that control in emergencies can be tricky. A good example is treating a bleeding patient. Every one of us has tied off a bleeder only to have another one erupt. You keep tying as fast as you can. When an emergency takes an unexpected turn, you turn with it.

This ability to respond to change is the result of training. Of course, some people just react and get lucky. But most of us can be taught to develop response ability that is agile, quick, and right on the mark.

PERSONAL STUDY EXERCISES

1. *Identify one thing about yourself that you would like to change.* Take responsibility for it, admitting that your circumstances are of your own choosing. Write down what you want to have happen. Plan action that will make it happen methodically within a given time frame. Be as specific as possible. Finally, do one thing right now that will move you toward your desired outcome.

2. *Write down the worst thing that could have happened in your last call.* How would you have handled it? What training could you do that might refine your skills at handling incidents like this imagined one? How would your colleagues have handled the imagined incident? What could you do together to train for such an incident?

3. *Take a look at the last time you made a mistake.* What happened that caused you to make the mistake? What information did you have? What information did you not have? What misinformation did you have? What did you interpret badly? What could have happened that would have caused you to make a different decision? What could you have done differently? What have you done or learned to make sure that you won't make the same mistake again? What would you do differently next time?

CHAPTER 5

Failure

"An empty bag cannot stand upright."

—Ben Franklin

A friend lost his business many years ago because of a litany of unfortunate mistakes. His problems started when an employee embezzled money because my friend had been sloppy in his bookkeeping practices and had trusted an employee he scarcely knew. Because his cash flow was destroyed by the embezzlement, he fell behind in paying his bills. Because he used all the cash he had to pay bills to try to keep the business open, he fell behind in paying his taxes. One thing led to another until the world came crashing down on him. He ended up in a tangle with creditors, vendors, and the IRS that eventually cost him his home, his business, and his sanity. When I asked him what had been the hardest part of all of it, he said simply, "I didn't know how to fail. All my life, I had been taught to succeed, but no one taught me how to fail."

Failure Is a Teacher

My friend may not have known how to fail, but I am going to teach you. First, let's define it. Simply put, failure is that awful moment when you realize that your efforts aren't going to yield the outcome you had planned. Failure is an incident; a mistake in judgment and action. I say that failure is a "mistake" because no one plans it. Failure does not describe or define a person. You aren't a failure just because you fail. Although it can be damaging, failure can be a good teacher, revealing many secrets about you, the people around you, and the circumstances that led to your mistake.

Every Great Mistake
Has a Halfway Moment

As mentioned above, author Pearl S. Buck wrote, "Every great mistake has a halfway moment, a split second when it can be recalled and perhaps remedied." But you'll never learn to recognize halfway moments unless you cross one or two. Of course, we both know that crossing a halfway moment means that you've passed the point of no return. You're into full-blown failure. This is what makes it a *great* mistake. In fact, the greater the mistake, the greater the lessons to be learned. It's important to fail so you'll learn where failure is.

Learning how to fail is an important part of learning how to be a great leader. Through failure, you certainly get to know yourself. But, better than that, you develop a more agile mind. When it doesn't occur to you that it's possible to fail, you can't think a situation through and develop fallback positions or bailouts. You don't look for "emergency exits" on your way into situations. This makes you dangerous. Understanding failure and considering it as a very real possibility will not only give you the ability to enter every situation with options, it will also help you to recognize impending failure in time for you to exercise those options. Let me give you an example. The successful leader—one who knows failure—is ordered to enter a burning warehouse with a team of firefighters. Because he knows that this is dangerous and they might not succeed in getting this fire under control before the floor caves in, he scans the warehouse for exits and builds safeguards into his strategies. He runs a mental inventory of everything he knows could go wrong and makes decisions in advance about how he's going to handle them. Before his team goes in, he makes sure everyone knows how they're going to get out, no matter what happens. He knows how to do this because he knows failure. He can recognize what Pearl S. Buck calls the "halfway moment" of the mistake. He knows it because he's crossed it and now knows where it is. A leader who has never experienced failure might lead that same team into the warehouse without planning for anything but success. With a cocky can-do attitude and the certainty that defeat is impossible, he might swashbuckle his way into disaster. When the floor starts to crumble, it's too late to start thinking about locating exits and counting firefighters. Dr. Karl E. Weick, noted author and expert on organizational behavior, says, "What we do not expect under life-threatening pressure is creativity."

Practice to Fail

Of course, those of us who work in emergency services can't fail on the job. It isn't acceptable to stand in the rubble and ruins amidst corpses and crow, "Hey! I now know where that halfway moment is! I crossed it!" The consequences of failure when you're responsible for life and property are devastating, and yet, you have to operate with a fundamental understanding of failure in order to be good at your job. In *Young Men and Fire,* author Norman Maclean writes that if the major purpose of your group is to "put out fires so fast they don't have time to become big ones," then you never learn much about fighting big fires. It's a conundrum, to be sure.

Since 1990, wildfires have claimed more than 23 firefighters' lives that might have been saved if they had dropped their tools to out-run the fire or had deployed their shelters to protect themselves. Psychologists and industry professionals have spent years analyzing the seemingly incomprehensible decisions that led to these deaths. The theories are complex and well published. But a central theme emerges among them all: These firefighters simply could not grasp the concept that they were failing. They were unable to recognize the halfway moment of the mistake. Because of this, they were unprepared to drop into "Plan B." They had no fallback positions. No escape plans. When the failure was fully upon them, this was clearly and certainly no time for creativity. Further, I think that when a firefighter is stubbornly melded to the idea that "Failure is impossible," he will take risks that are foolish. The peril is compounded. Now, not only will the firefighter launch into deadly territory without an escape plan, he will also have no clue that the situation has gone past the point of no return. Worse than that, he will seldom be alone at the time.

The trick to mastering failure *without* getting killed and destroying civilization as we know it is that you have to *practice* crossing those pesky halfway moments. Fortunately for you, emergency services provides ample opportunity for simulation training. Unfortunately for you, your trainers are teaching you to do everything perfectly so that your outcomes will be successful. It might be up to you to take your training one step further and add "Failure 101" to your personal curriculum.

Dr. Weick suggests that an effective strategy for putting failure into your experience is to "overtrain to failure." The benefits will be twofold. First, you'll learn to recognize halfway moments, and second, you'll learn that failure is success when it saves your life. Play the game "What If?" Take every training exercise and make the longest, most creative list of possible disastrous outcomes you can. Let's say you're hauling a hose. What if you trip and fall on your face? What if a truck runs over the hose and crushes it? What if the water cuts off? What if the hose wraps around a post? What if it's freezing at the fire scene and your hands are too cold to work? What if you suddenly find yourself standing in a pool of gasoline? What if a fellow firefighter collapses right in front of you? What if the building you're soaking explodes? What if? What if? What if? Of course, postulating is good, but *practicing* is even better. Like Dr. Weick says, "overtrain to failure." Simulating your response to failure will sharpen your skill and deepen your instincts. Remember, sometimes when disaster strikes, you respond from your gut. Your instincts take over. You react without thinking. If your reaction is one that you've practiced in simulation, your chances are better that you'll drop right into your Plan B rather than waste precious seconds trying to intellectualize, analyze, and search for creative solutions. At the halfway moment, there aren't any.

Coming to Terms With Failure

Practicing failure doesn't make it any less real. There will come a time in your life when you really, truly fail. The only thing sudden about failure is that awful moment when you realize that it has you in its stranglehold. Indeed, failure happens in slow motion, often methodically. Later, when you honestly, privately, microscopically examine the failure (and you will!), you'll no doubt discover far too many ways that it should have been recognized and could have been averted. I call this "Singing the Shoulda-Coulda Blues." The tune goes something like this:

1. Sickening Realization. There's no one among us who doesn't know this feeling. It's that nauseating moment when you realize that something has gone horribly wrong. Apparently, all your efforts have been in vain. You did your best. All that you knew, all that you did, and all that you hoped for were not enough to pull it off. In spite of your intentions, plans, and efforts, "it" is going to crash and burn. I call it the "Sickening Realization" because I have known grown men literally to throw up at this moment.

2. Denial. No matter how cool and professional you are on the outside, inside you are screaming, "Oh, no! This can't be happening!" You scramble for ways to reinterpret the harsh emergence of truth, to see if you can find a way to resculpt the facts into a more acceptable outcome. You assume that your information is inaccurate or incomplete, so you dive at it again and again, hoping for a different outcome each time. This is why, when you hear bad news, you predictably respond, "WHAT?!" All humans do. When we first hear something we don't like, we demand to have it clarified, as if we couldn't possibly have heard it right the first time. After a while, if you're at all intelligent, truth finally sinks in. You've failed.

3. Frantic Search for a Bailout. Overwhelmed by evidence that failure is imminent (if not right on you), you spring into action, building barricades and plugging up holes. If the situation looks hopeless, perhaps it only seems hopeless. Maybe there's something you can do to make it less so. Maybe you can change your approach to achieve the same outcome. Or one that is similar. The battle cry for this struggle is "BUT IF . . . BUT IF . . . BUT IF . . ." This phase of the process is accompanied by desperate emotional and mental acrobatics, plus frenzied activity. You have to try to salvage the situation. You just have to.

4. Shock. Like being struck by 100,000 volts of electricity, there comes a moment when you're suddenly jolted by the reality and finality of the failure. For an instant, the shock paralyzes you, stops your heart, and takes your breath away. Although this is undeniably the worst, most painful, and most chilling moment in singing the "Coulda-Shoulda Blues," it is also the one that signals "Hey, buddy, let the healing begin!"

5. *Blame.* It might be the moment to begin healing, but you would be less than human if you didn't first cast around, looking for someone or something to blame for your failure. No one likes to admit that he is wrong and capable of acts of monumental stupidity. (Although thinking that you're wrong or stupid might be totally off base, this is what failure looks and feels like at this step in the process.) In fact, the harder you try to succeed, the more you need to blame. You simply must scan the universe for people or circumstances to hang this failure on. You need to be let off the hook, even if only a little. Sometimes you'll find a partner in crime or a circumstance that did, in fact, contribute to the failure. Sometimes you'll come to the grudging conclusion that you screwed up all by yourself. Sometimes you'll discover that, although people and circumstances were significant factors, in the end you were in control. You'll conclude, as we all do, that blame is a useless waste of time.

6. *Acceptance.* Acceptance of failure requires that you take three important steps: (1) accept the reality of the situation; (2) accept the irrevocability of the failure; and finally (3) accept your responsibility in it. You're never going to be able to get over it or learn a thing from it if you never deal with it. When you're ready, you have to surrender. See the situation as it really is. Very simply, you tried. You failed. Period. End of story. Wave that white flag and come out of your foxhole. Nothing you can do is going to change the fact that you failed. It's your responsibility.

7. *Action.* Failure, once discovered, rarely just lies there. You can't just walk away and pretend that it doesn't exist. Failure demands some resolution. Once you accept and understand the failure and the situation created by it, you have to take steps to fix it, in both the short and long term. Right now, you need to set things straight, and you need to learn enough from the failure to avoid similar failures in the future.

How to Go On Living

Failure isn't the measure of anyone. How a person handles that failure is. We have discussed dealing with failure. But when it's all said and done, then you have to go on living. Here are some strategies for picking yourself up and dusting yourself off.

1. *Welcome to the human race!* We would all like to be perfect all the time, but in truth, we're all flawed and we all make mistakes. Being flawed and making mistakes are part of being human. If you're like most of us, you do the best you can. Failure doesn't define you. If you ran your Big Red Truck into a light pole, it means simply that you ran your Big Red Truck into a light pole. It doesn't mean anything more than that. It isn't possible to extrapolate all sorts of conclusions from that one momentary lapse in your life. You will not henceforth be known as the One Who Runs Big Red Trucks Into Light Poles. A failure doesn't wipe your slate clean of all that you have accomplished and con- tributed in your whole life. Remember that failing doesn't make you a failure. That's the good news. The bad news is that you're going to have to take some guff for your actions and you'll have to live with the failure for the rest of your life, but there will be a "rest of your life" with lots more for you to accomplish and con- tribute. If you think you're being judged harshly, realize that you're being judged by other human beings, all of whom have experienced failure, some lots worse than yours. So cut yourself some slack. Besides, if you were perfect, you would be annoying and have no friends.

2. *Realize that you made the best decisions you could make with the information you had available at the time.* We have a tendency, when analyzing failure, to relive the events and circumstances that led to the failure over and over and over until we forget that hindsight is nearly always 20/20. Oh, sure. It's all crystal clear to you now. But, if you'll back off, you'll realize that many things that are painfully obvious to you right this minute weren't visible at all when you were trying to make decisions earlier. People do the best they can. You're no exception. When you make a decision, you collect and examine all the data you have on hand at the time. If you have bad information or interpret good information badly, your decision will reflect flawed assumptions. Certainly you could get lucky and make a good decision accidentally, but it's unlikely. In your life- time, you've made thousands of great decisions. You'll make thou- sands more. In this one instance, you blew it. Now you have more information. Next time you'll do better.

3. *Do everything possible to make the situation right.* Self-respect demands that you right a wrong. Not all situations can be "fixed," but all situations have avenues of restitution. Sometimes failure is personal, private, and invisible to everyone but you. For example, you decided to clean behind the refrigerator, and then forgot to buy cleanser, scheduled an appointment over the time you set aside for the big cleaning, and discovered that you couldn't move the refrigerator anyway. You failed to get that job done, but no one but you knows that you had planned to do it. The failure is minor and private. The only one disappointed in you is you. However, when you fail as a leader, other people are almost always involved, and worse, adversely affected. So your restitution probably involves having to make amends. How you do so depends on the situation. Restitution could run the gamut from paying back money to living the rest of your life under a solemn personal oath that you'll NEVER DO THAT AGAIN. When I think of restitution by oath, I think of Ebenezer Scrooge from Charles Dickens' *A Christmas Carol.* Mr. Scrooge was a miserable failure of a human being. He was cold and miserly. When the ghosts of Christmases past, present, and future took him on a late-night ride and showed him how he had gone wrong, Mr. Scrooge mended his wicked ways. He spent the rest of his life being generous and loving, conducting his personal and professional affairs in an exemplary manner. He couldn't right every past wrong, but he could avoid making future mistakes. Sometimes oath-taking is the best one can do.

4. *Fully examine and understand the nature of the failure so that you won't repeat the same mistakes again.* It's important that you fully understand your failure. Only then will you understand what you're supposed to learn from it. This is one examination that I ask you to conduct alone. Other people will undoubtedly be glad to give you their opinions (whether or not you ask), but their insight into your situation is limited to what they know. You know more. Besides, it's nearly impossible to keep yourself from leaping into a defensive mode when someone is happily reeling off the list of your many faults and all the stupid things you did that led up to this failure. When you feel defensive, you speak with less than candor and you

listen to less than truth. It's natural to put up all your shields. If you really want to see all sides of the situation, you have to look into yourself and ask some really tough questions:

Your defensive self says, "I didn't cause this failure."
Your honest self should ask, "Really, did I have nothing to do with it?"

Your defensive self says, "I tried everything."
Your honest self should ask, "Trying isn't the same thing as doing. Was there more I should have done? What was it?"

Your defensive self says, "I did everything I could think of to make this a success."
Your honest self should ask, "Really, did I do everything? Was there anything I thought of but didn't do? What was it?"

Here's the killer question that could keep you awake all night:

Your defensive self says, "In spite of my efforts, I failed."
Your honest self should ask, "Did I fail on purpose? Did I fail because I set myself up to fail? Was there something about failing that was easier than succeeding? What did I fear more than failure? What did I do to cause this? Why?"

5. *Ask for forgiveness.* When your failure impacts another person, you owe him or her an apology. This can be really tough, because your failure was unintentional, even accidental. It's safe to assume that you never meant to hurt anyone else. It doesn't matter. If another person is involved, his disappointment—no matter how small—will haunt you. It's important to stand up to your responsibility in the situation and take it on the chin. Tell the person what happened as honestly and in as much detail as you can. Then stand quietly and allow the person to speak. Even if the other person rants and raves, resist the urge to throw yourself onto the defensive. You'll know you're slipping if you start your next sentence with "Yeah, but . . ." Stop, pal. You need to hear this. And the other person needs to have the opportunity to communicate displeasure. At the end of your discussion, ask for forgiveness. Say, "I understand.

I'm sorry. I did my best. Please forgive me." Ninety-nine times out of a hundred, the other person will let you off the hook.

6. *Forgive other people involved.* If, in fact, there were other people involved in your having failed, get over it—now. Remember that we are all flawed and human. We all do the best we can. We all make decisions by considering information we have on hand at the time. Bad information yields bad decisions. Millions of things at any moment can go wrong in a chaotic universe. Harboring resentment and anger will only harm you. It's better to chalk up the failure to experience. You'll be smarter next time you deal with people.

Besides, when you swiftly let other people off the hook and seize responsibility for the failure as your own, you're in a position to fix the situation or make restitution. As long as you think that you're not in charge and continue to chant, "It's not my fault! It's not my fault!" you have no control or power. You'll never discover the lessons or receive any of the benefits from learning them. Finally, people who watch you waste your time seething over the short-comings of others will lose respect for you. Why is it your responsibility to forgive those people responsible for your failure? Because if they helped you cause it, they feel as badly as you do. Maybe worse. Forgiveness heals everyone—they and you.

7. *Forgive yourself.* As a responsible person, forgiving yourself is a whole lot more difficult than forgiving other people. You'll go through the old "I could kick myself!" routine. You'll lie awake nights. You'll simmer and stew in your own juices. Your confidence will be shot. You'll have difficulty making decisions. (Heaven forbid that you might be wrong again!) You'll stop taking risks. (Better to do nothing than do something that might be wrong again!) You have to break this cycle before it begins. Step outside yourself for a moment and ask, "Could I forgive friends for failing?" The answer is, "Of course." Then be as good a friend to yourself as you are to everyone (anyone!) else. Forgive yourself.

8. *Resolve to do everything possible to keep from making the same mistakes in the future.* The failure is complete *only* if you learn nothing from it. There are great lessons within even the smallest failure. At

worst, you've learned what *not* to do if you want to avoid repeating the same mistakes that led to failure. At best, you've gathered tools and insight that will help you not only to avoid repeating mistakes, but also to build more solid plans in the future. Some people fail and are paralyzed by the fear that it will happen again. These suddenly cautious, careful people have my personal assurance that they will never fail again. Indeed, people who never try never fail. Of course, they also will never accomplish one more thing in life. It's over. Other people fail and are made fearless by the experience. They figure that they've seen the worst and it wasn't so bad.

Maybe next time, they'll succeed. Life is all about taking risks and trying things. Some things don't work out exactly the way you planned, but you try again. Hey, win a few, lose a few!

9. *Dust yourself off. Life goes on.* The sun rises every morning and sets every evening. You have no choice but to keep on living. You have to find a way. It's naive to think that any failure can be overcome by a simple decision to "get on with it." The more catastrophic the results of your failure, the longer it might take you to learn to live with it. But you will.

10. *Get back in the game.* Not only does life go on, it also requires your participation. If your confidence is so shaken by failure that you can't make any more big decisions, start back with little ones. Nothing breeds success like success. Think back to all the things in your life that turned out perfectly, and realize that your decisions and actions were right on the mark. One failure neither discounts all of your accomplishments nor wipes out all your skill and talent. Everything is still intact. Go for it.

The Gifts of Failure

From our earliest childhood, we were all taught the undeniable superiority of success. We spent every recess playing competitive games where there were winners (those who succeeded) and losers (those who failed). When I think about my first introduction to the glorious, golden benefits of success, I think about the playground and baseball. Every afternoon, we would divide ourselves into two teams: "theirs" and "ours." Taking turns, we chose up sides by selecting the most skilled players for ourselves. We avoided having to select the dorks until the final rounds, when there were no more choices. We thoughtfully and strategically assigned ourselves and our teammates to positions where we performed best and were sure to clobber the other team. We assigned the dorks to positions where they could do the least harm. Every time our team did something good, our little self-appointed cheering section exploded, hooting and hollering their deafening approval. Being given a standing ovation for every little accomplishment was a compelling, intoxicating incentive to succeed. On the flip side, whenever we performed woefully, our cheering section groaned or (worse) sat sullen-faced and silent. Even when you're little, it doesn't take long to learn that success is good and failure is bad. It's an unfortunate lesson when you're trying to learn about life, because success teaches you very little and failure teaches you a lot. Frankly, you have to hit a few bad balls to learn how to nail a home run. You have to let a few grounders slip past you to learn how to rocket out and catch one. I remember the disdain with which we would mock the grownups' chant: "Remember, boys and girls. It's not whether you win or lose. It's how you play the game that counts." Yeah, right. Even grownups couldn't have believed that. We kids sure didn't. I never saw the opposing team jumping up and down, cheering after we had creamed them: "Yay! We lost, but we played the best we could! Go, team!" I think it is more honest to say, "Winning isn't the important thing. It's the *only* thing."

But being honest isn't being right. In fact, winning isn't everything. Succeeding is. When winning is so important to you that you take unnecessary risks and deny the possibility of failure to the detriment of your ability to plan properly, you seriously move yourself and the people who count on you toward disaster. In emergency services, you have to learn to make distinctions between winning and succeeding. Start now. "Failure is a great teacher best met early in life." Surviving a crushing failure teaches you one of the most important lessons that you'll ever learn. Simply, life goes on. The earlier you learn it, the longer you and the people you lead will have benefit of it.

Failure Clears a Path for Success

When I think of people who have failed, I am reminded of the true story of a man who couldn't seem to do anything right. He attended school only intermittently as he was growing up, but he was highly ambitious. As a young man, he threw his hat into the ring for the Illinois General Assembly but lost the election. So he enlisted in the military, was assigned to a rifle company, and achieved the rank of captain. Unfortunately, his company disbanded, necessitating his reenlistment as a private. Back to square one. After serving in the military, he returned home to work in a store that subsequently went out of business. So he bought a store of his own with a partner. It too failed, leaving him badly in debt. His partner died a year later, plunging him further into debt. His sweetheart died the following year. He had a nervous breakdown. After he recovered, he made a bid for the U.S. Congress. He lost the election. He tried again and was elected to the Illinois legislature, but declined the seat in order to run for the U.S. Senate. He lost the election. Then he was nominated to run as the candidate for Republican senator from Illinois, but lost the election after stunning and now-famous (and humiliatingly public) debates with his opponent. What a loser! Right? Wrong. This man who couldn't seem to do anything right was Abraham Lincoln. As you know, in 1860 he was elected as the 16th and first Republican U.S. President. And his list of accomplishments is etched in our history as among the most important and significant made by any leader.

PERSONAL STUDY EXERCISES

1. Play the "What If" game by applying at least potential difficulties to the task in which you're the most competent.

2. Examine the worst failure of your life and make a list of three things you did to cause it.

3. Examine the worst failure of your life and make a list of three important things it taught you.

CHAPTER 6

Step Down to Step Up

"The doors of wisdom are never shut."

—Ben Franklin

G one are the days when orders were hurled like lightning bolts down from Mount Olympus on blindly obedient firefighters and EMTs who lived to satisfy the whims of faceless, uniformed gods and goddesses. Today, our leaders are in the trenches; the orders of old have been replaced by decisions we reach together; nothing whimsical appears unexpectedly; and the faces of leadership are familiar. The new leaders are partners, not deities.

Leaders as Humans

I witnessed one of the first moments of this new paradigm when I was a young firefighter. A battalion chief who hadn't been on the street in a long time sent a surprise memo to the station, ordering us to place the trauma kits on the No. 1 side of the engine and to seat the third person on the engine on the No. 2 side. Lightning bolt having been hurled, it was now up to us to figure out how to maintain efficiency when, on calls, the third person had to leap off and completely circumnavigate the engine to get to the equipment. Being dutiful, we obeyed the order. Being intelligent, we searched for the logic. We justified his memo with, "He must have had a good reason. Maybe we're too inexperienced to figure out what he had in mind here. He knows more than we do. He is, after all, the battalion chief." But after a few chaotic calls, someone uttered the ultimate heresy: "Maybe the chief doesn't know what he's talking about." It was a startling thought. We knew we couldn't continue arriving on life-and-death calls and then waste precious time running around (literally). Desperate to restore order, we phoned the chief and invited him to come to the station to ride the engines and have a personal look at his new procedures in action. Then we collectively held our breath. Would he blow his stack at our bold insubordination? Would he stubbornly cling to his mandates even in the face of overwhelming evidence that he had made a mistake? Or would he be mature enough to correct it? Fortunately for us, the chief was about to evolve into one of the first generation "New Leaders." He only went out on one call. When he observed the inefficiency he had caused by issuing orders without sufficient information or experience, he immediately rescinded them. He didn't offer an apology, and we didn't ask for one. We were just relieved that procedures were once again on an even keel and our third person could retire his track shoes! Still, something unexpected and wonderful happened in our respectful exchange. Our dialogue taught him a couple of things. First, we held a wealth of information that we were eager to make available to him. Second, he needed to spend more time in the trenches with us to get back in touch with basics and with people. The view from his ivory tower may have afforded him a panoramic perspective, but he couldn't see the details. Leadership is not a spectator sport. We learned that leaders—even battalion chiefs—are indeed human.

When You Admit You're Human

One of the key roles of a leader is to steer an organization and its people through transitions. This has never been more difficult than it is today. Emergency services, by their very nature, are performed in a chaotic work environment. Add to that the rapidly changing faces of governments, clashing cultures, colliding value systems, financial pinches, threats of litigation, emerging technologies, and evolving partnerships with other agencies, and you've got a challenge on your hands. Being able not only to survive but to thrive requires thinking on your toes and acting even faster. Fortunately, you're trained to do that, and so are all the people with whom you work.

Let's be honest. You don't know it all and you never will. The world is moving much too fast for you to have all the answers. You're lucky if you have even a few. If two heads are better than one, you can bet that a whole stationful of people is better than two. When you're an accessible leader who respects the partnership of your coworkers, then you're free to seek counsel. Other people's input will surprise you, as will the depth of information and experience that they bring to your decisions.

Seeking counsel, however, isn't easy. It means that you're going to have to admit right out loud that you don't have all the answers. Not having all the answers means that you lack knowledge and experience, that you're unsure, and that you're not in full control of the situation. It sounds bad, doesn't it? In reality, whether it's bad or good depends on your role in the organization. It depends on whether you're the leader or merely a manager. If you see yourself as a manager, then seeking counsel might make you feel like a total failure. Remember, as a manager, your job is to carry out orders through the efforts of other people. Managing is how a job gets done. Certainly, wavering over how to do a job could be interpreted as incompetent. On the other hand, *leading* is determining what the mission is and why the job gets done. As a leader, when you realize and admit that you need help, you instantly put yourself in position to galvanize your organization, to draw people to your purpose. With their input and consensus, your mission becomes our mission. Now, you lead.

It's important to understand that the key to leadership is not in running around and whining for help. It is, however, in a quiet attitude of accessibility, an open mind, and an open door. You're a human being. You know it. The people who work with you know it. You'll be a better leader when you operate from a position of integrity, when you're real and authentic.

So, How Do You Let People Know You're One of Them?

The trick in being a facile leader today is to lead from the bottom, where the trenches are. Picture the standard organizational chart. The boss is at the top. Under him are top-level managers. Under those people are middle-level managers. Under middle managers are the workers. Under the workers are support staff such as janitors. When it's all drawn out, it is a distinct pyramid with the boss at the pinnacle and all the underlings spreading out beneath the golden throne. Visualizing an organization by delineating the employees and lining them all up is a good way to get the whole picture and to see where you fit into the scheme of things. The problem is that this traditional organizational chart is upside down. One simple flip and you've got it right. As a leader, you should be under your people, supporting them and making it possible for them to do their best work. When you're supporting people rather than perching on top of them, you create an environment that's safe for people to exercise their creativity and use their experience to benefit the whole group. When people on each level see their mission as supporting people on the level right above them, then the organization assumes a culture of caring and enabling. And their attitude toward you will be that of respectful partnership. After all, you're there to take care of them so they can do their best. You're accessible. You're in touch with reality. You're in the trenches as low as you can get so that your organization can balance on your shoulders.

Tips for Communicating Person to Person

You've had millions of successful, lively conversations in your life, but something paralyzing happens in the workplace when the person with whom you're trying to speak takes one look at your rank and panics. Yet, in spite of the difficulty, you need input from people at work. How do you overcome the problems that seem to plague a leader trying to enter into conversation? I talk a lot about listening in the next chapter, but there are a few tips that will help you be an accessible human being and a better leader. Before I tell you how to behave, please know that I am aware that this behavior could be construed as manipulative and insincere. I urge you to keep your integrity intact and to approach all human interaction with sincerity and honesty.

1. *Get in front of people.* No one will realize that you are human and open to conversation if they don't know you exist. Nothing sparks communication better than a face-to-face encounter between two people, so get out of your office, descend from your ivory tower, and

get out on the floor. I've already told you that you have to be in the trenches with your company. Indeed, the more people see you, the more comfortable they'll be around you. Familiarity doesn't breed contempt. It breeds comfort. People get to know you and trust you, and before you know it, you've got a connection.

Open the conversation with a friendly greeting, and get the person to talk to you with an open-ended question. This is a technique that has been finely honed by talk show hosts who are skilled at filling airtime with conversation. They say that one surefire way to kill a conversation dead in its tracks is to ask a question to which the answer is yes or no.

Let me give you an example. A conversation-killer question might be: "Is the apparatus handling okay?" The death-blow answer is "Yes." A more effective, open-ended question and one that will generate conversation on the same topic is: "If you had to make one significant adjustment to the apparatus, what would it be?" This forces the person to think and then string more than a couple of words together. This is the beginning of a dialogue.

2. *Make eye contact.* While you're interacting, maintain eye contact. If you're looking around when someone is talking, you send a loud, clear signal that you're bored and distracted. If you're wearing sunglasses, take them off. When you maintain eye contact, you demonstrate your presence in the conversation and your attentiveness to what the person is saying. Additionally, you are able to help the other person stay in the conversation. In our culture, it's difficult to break away from unwavering eye contact and wander off from the conversation.

Making eye contact gives the person with whom you are speaking instantaneous feedback. By allowing him to read your face without attempting to mask your reactions, the person is given assurance that you're being real. By the way, you get the same benefit.

3. *Listen carefully without interrupting.* One reason that coworkers are reluctant to tell you what they think is that they fear being judged by you. Frankly, they don't want you to think they're stupid or behaving inappropriately. In any organization, a lot of unspoken rules govern the relationships between people of different professional ranking. Many of these rules dictate strict decorum in com-

munication, and all the rules give the upper hand to the higher-ranking person. Although there are lots of rules, let me give you an example of two in action: An employee can't criticize a boss, and an employee cannot dictate a boss's behavior. It's strictly against the rules for an employee to say to a boss, "You really blew this assignment. You have to stay late to fix it. Have it corrected and on my desk in the morning when I get here." It wouldn't matter if the employee's work depended on the boss's delivery of a perfect assignment, and the boss's inability to deliver had directly violated an agreement they'd made. The employee would be bound to silence by the rules. On the other hand, a boss might very easily and appropriately say to an employee, "You really blew this assignment. You have to stay late to fix it. Have it corrected and on my desk in the morning when I get here." The unspoken threat—the consequence of balking at the criticism or violating this mandate—is being fired. Herein lies the real power—management by intimidation—and the reason that the rules work in favor of only the higher-ranked person. As long as one person has the power to fire another person, they are not equals. Their conversation will reflect this.

Until now. When it's a leader's mission to make the workplace a safe environment for those who work there, then the threat of firing—or any lesser consequence—is eliminated. That's your job now. In conversing with a coworker of any rank, you have to allow him to say whatever needs to be said. Your job is to listen without invoking any of the unspoken rules that will shut down communication. Be a human being conversing with a human being. Be without judgment. Be open. Listen.

4. *React and respond.* I tell you to listen, but I also warn you that conversation is a two-way street. Sooner or later, you'll have to talk, too. You're not conducting a survey. You don't get to launch that one really good open-ended question, stare deeply into your partner's eyes, and then just sit there in stone silence. No. You have to react and respond. This is, after all, a conversation. In breaking the ice with coworkers, however, I caution you to keep your reactions and responses on a positive level. Remember that one false move from you will remind your partner that you are indeed "above" him. In one instant, all real communication will fade behind the

rules, and you'll be left with nothing except platitudes and secrecy. Therefore, you have to remember that the purpose of this conversation is twofold. First, you are making honest contact with a fellow human being. Second, and equally important, you're retraining an entire company to ditch the rules and learn to trust each other.

5. *Thank the person.* When a coworker has been honest with you, remember to close the conversation with a heartfelt thank-you. You're grateful not only for the ideas your partner shared but also that this person had the courage and trusted you enough to lay aside the rules for a moment. He did so at great personal and professional risk from you and peers, who might interpret your conversation as betrayal (the old "us-them" stuff). To some extent, you were allowed into the heart of another human being. It is necessary to honor that with a verbal acknowledgment. No need to get gushy. Just say something like, "Thank you for taking the time to talk to me about this. I really appreciate it."

6. *Make a vow to yourself that there will be no retribution or punishment for that person's input.* No matter what your partner said in the conversation, never let him regret it. Never punish. Never betray. Never. When you draw another person into communication, you are retraining that person to disobey the rules, to trust you a little, and to take a huge risk. When your partner agrees to all this and speaks openly, you are being retrained to park your power at the door for a while. Remember, two people are not equal as long as one person has the power to fire, and like it or not, you are that person. If you ask your partner to ignore that fact, then you, too, have to ignore it.

7. *Be careful how you recount the conversation.* Stations are small places. Gossip is a favorite pastime. If you have a conversation with a coworker and you recount the conversation to someone else, you can bet your bottom dollar that it's going to get back to the coworker. Along its way back to the source, that conversation is going to filter through other people. For this reason, if you choose to speak of the conversation, you'd better be careful what you say. If you tell Joe that you spoke with Sally and she poured her heart out to you but that you could barely contain your urge to gag at what an idiot she

is, it will only be a matter of time before Sally hears about it. Again, I warn you that Sally won't be the only audience for your unattractive editorial. Other people will hear it, too. They'll know that you think Sally is an idiot, but worse, they'll know that you betrayed her confidence and that you're laughing at her behind her back. It will be a cold day in hell before they talk to you. It would be far better to govern your words. Be careful about what you say. Speak of the conversation, even in private, with respect and gratitude.

8. *Give credit where credit is due.* When someone gives you information that you use, you have to give credit where credit is due. When you use someone's idea and don't give credit, in effect you steal the idea. Word will spread that you aren't to be trusted. Intense resentment will build. In the past, stealing ideas might have been the stock and trade of unscrupulous management, but it has no place in a safe work environment where men and women are valued. If someone helps you, say so. Say so as publicly as possible without embarrassing anyone. Give credit where credit is due. If a project works out brilliantly, you will not be diminished in the least by giving recognition to those who made it happen. As a leader, your job is to support them, to make it possible for them to shine. Obviously, you may do this very well even if your name appears nowhere on the project.

9. *If you listen to advice but don't use it, you owe an explanation.* You can't use all of the information you'll be given. Someday someone will come to you with an idea so far-fetched that you'll want to laugh out loud. You'll sober up, however, when you realize that now you have to let this person down gently. Follow all the tips I've given you for being a good and supportive listener, but be honest. Explain in as much detail as you can that you think the idea won't work. One of two things will happen. Either the person will realize that he didn't have as much information as you do and completely understand your reasoning, or a dialogue will begin. When the person has the same information you do, the idea can be explored in a new context. You might be surprised at the outcome. Whatever happens, remember to thank the person sincerely. Leave the communication conduit wide open for next time. If you handle it right, there will be a next time.

10. *Remember that success begets success.* Every step you take toward open communication—human being to human being—brings you closer to success as a leader. It won't be easy. There will be setbacks as you and everyone around you learns to trust, but the result is worth the effort.

The Difference Between a Trench and a Foxhole

If you're going to be in the trenches, you have to get muddy. You can't fake being real by wandering in and out of the workplace, smiling and shaking hands. Management experts call this "walking." It's as superficial as it sounds. No one is deceived. In fact, employees can spot a walker a mile away and have no respect for the act. Walking doesn't support anyone or create a safe culture in the organization. All it does is wear out shoe leather. Walking is the act of a coward who's too threatened by his own vulnerability to allow an employee to get close. Rather than getting down in the trenches, a walker digs a foxhole for protection and climbs in. On the other hand, walking can be a spectacular first step as long as all the steps that follow are authentic, genuine, and honest. If you're trying to break out of the traditional us-them management mold and become a true leader who supports employees, then it's necessary to step down out of that ivory tower and make a human connection.

Let's make an important distinction. Employees work *with* you. They don't work *for* you. Once you understand the nature of your dependence on each other, then your roles become clear.

Experts tell us that an important step in making the human connection is to tear down the barriers imposed by separate dining rooms, reserved parking spaces, and secluded offices and sleeping quarters. Of course, there are appropriate times and places for privacy, confidentiality, and security, but these should be judiciously used. When you're not handling sensitive matters, you need to be in the thick of things, making certain that you're doing everything just right to make it possible for people to do their best work.

Leadership Is Not a Spectator Sport

Experts tell us that today's effective leader is *in* the game, not hanging over the top of it looking down. They warn us that placing a leader on a pedestal—or having the leader climb up there on his own—creates dangerous impediments in our ability to communicate with one another. The distance between top and bottom is simply too far for shouting. No one can hear the words, and the messages get garbled. The leader who is poised on a lofty perch quickly loses touch with the challenges and problems that are reality for the rest of the people in the organization. The people who are below the pedestal tend to dehumanize the aloof leader. There is no real empathy. No real understanding. Certainly no communication. Remember my story about the out-of-touch battalion chief who issued the memo ordering those of us in the station to place the trauma kits on the No. 1 side of the engine and seat the third person on the engine on the No. 2 side? Even though we were able to get him to change his mind fairly quickly, in today's leadership environment, that might never have happened at all. I, as a lower ranking officer, would have had immediate access to him no matter where he was in our organizational chart. The chief would have been in direct contact with us, especially before he thought about making changes in how we operated. We each would have been accustomed to dialogue and discussion before decisions were made and directives were issued. Looking back on the incident, I realize now that much of our failure at the time was my fault and the fault of my peers. We didn't help the chief—or anyone ranked above us—stay in touch with our situation at the station. We, like all young firefighters, let them stay perched on their pedestals, looking down. At the time, we didn't know how to invite them down.

In emergency services, particularly where labor unions are involved, the old us-them mentality pervades the company. There can be a real sense of distance between the upper echelon and the rest of us. Indeed, simply referring to management as the upper echelon implies that employees are low on the totem pole, far below our officers. Admit it. When you speak of "us," you are seldom talking about the whole organization. You are selectively referring to your peers. If you speak of "them," you don't even have to define the reference. If you're in the lower ranks, you are talking about management. "We" have to inspect hydrants this week. "They" sent the orders. If you're in management, "they" refers to lower-ranking troops. It's this us-them mentality that makes rising through the ranks so difficult. The actual effort of earning a promotion might not be so tough, but adjusting from spending your career as an "us" and then becoming one of the dreaded "them" can be daunting. In the past, to become an officer meant severing loyalty from one group and aligning with another. The aspiring officer had to detach from brothers in the organization to become "management." With access to the employees suddenly limited, the officer had to rely on old experience. This worked for a while, but information became obsolete in an alarmingly short time. Replenishing information was difficult, because communications conduits were no longer as effective as they were when the new officer and the employees were peers. The relationship eroded further, and communication conduits became even less effective. Every mistake the leader made was seized by employees as evidence of increasing incompetence. Every decision was suspect. This, of course, was the scenario in the old, traditional structure.

Today's leader doesn't work within an us-them paradigm. Indeed, if "we're all in this together," "we" means "everyone." The effective leader, even though promoted, does not sever ties with his coworkers. On the contrary, those ties are strengthened through ongoing dialogue and accessibility. Through the newly promoted officer, the coworkers have greater access to information and input. Their power is increased. They also know they have a strong advocate in this leader who has personal experience with the challenges they face every day. The entire organization works hard to keep communication open so that everyone is in touch and in tune with the mission. The outcome is radically different from the traditional us-them system, which breeds suspicion and secrecy. New leadership fosters a safe, supportive environment.

The Fine Line Between Bosses and Buddies

Now that I've told you that you need to mingle and seek counsel, let me assure you that I understand that it's possible to get too buddy-buddy with people in your organization. Your ability to make an impartial decision may be impaired. Also, it's possible that your constant presence might be confused for friendship that could obscure the lines of command when it's necessary for you to pull rank. Without a doubt, there's a fine line between "enough" and "too much" togetherness. You'll find that balance, perhaps by crossing the line a time or two. When I was an 18-year-old volunteer firefighter in Meadeville, Pennsylvania, we got a call to respond to a fire at the telephone company warehouse. Charlie Allen was in charge. A group of us were up on the roof, ventilating it. Charlie shouted up at us from the ground to get off the roof right away. I remember shouting back down to my friend, "Just settle down! We're almost done and we're doing fine!" The next thing I knew, Charlie was up on the ladder, screaming in our faces, "Get down! Now!" We followed him down the ladder just as the steel girders warped. Charlie, from his perspective underneath us, could see what we couldn't see—that conditions were changing and the building was becoming unstable. His orders had changed to match the changing situation. Charlie clearly was doing his job as a leader who provided us with support and a safe environment for doing our best. The problem was that the order to abandon the roof came not only from Charlie our leader but also our friend. Our challenge to his order wasn't out of disrespect. The challenge was issued because we mistakenly assumed that all our decisions could be made by consensus. If we thought good old Charlie was overreacting, we were within our rights to tell him to chill out and let us finish our jobs. It was a huge mistake that nearly cost us our lives, but it taught us all a lesson. Charlie reaffirmed his authority with a stern lecture and a subsequent (slight) pullback in familiarity. And we learned to make fine distinctions between "friend" and "leader." It was an important lesson for an 18-year-old. Finding that balance is difficult but necessary. People with whom you work have to know you're human, but they also have to understand that part of your job is to move the organization forward by your authority. If you strike that balance, people will perceive your leadership as being logical and a direct result of their input. If you fail to strike the balance, you could find yourself on a ladder, screaming at a confused 18-year-old about to fall through a roof.

Leadership Isn't a Job

You don't have to be a boss to be a leader. Experts in human behavior point out that leadership is not a job or a title conferred on you. Leadership is a state of being. It comes from within a person who develops it. Leadership emerges on its own, sometimes from the most surprising places. It's entirely possible for a rookie to emerge as a leader with more influence and power than a veteran chief. If you're a leader, you won't wait until you're promoted to start eliminating barriers, seeking counsel, and being an authentic human being. You will have been doing that all the while before someone ever hands you a new rank.

Well before you're promoted, eliminate the narrow thinking that forces you into an us-them mentality. When you catch yourself being lazy and referring to coworkers as "us" or managers as "them," STOP. Back up and be more specific about who you're talking about. Use names. If you observe a higher-ranking officer making a mistake, realize that this is a human being—flawed and yet doing the best that he can. Break the us-them paradigm mold. Offer to help. Make the gesture with maturity, compassion, integrity, and sincerity. If you are rebuffed, understand that the officer thinks of himself as management and is threatened by your perception that things are not in full control. That officer has been conditioned to think that you should never see imperfections. The effort to maintain this illusion has been exhausting, but there is no way in the us-them paradigm for the officer to let you cross over from your camp to theirs. Never mind. Next time, you might succeed. When your offer to help is accepted and you do cross over, you'll be seen as a turncoat or a brownnoser by peers who won't understand your apparent defection. You'll have to explain and defend your actions. Great! Here is your opportunity to teach your peers about "all of us being in this together." My advice is to deliver the message with a light, matter-of-fact touch. Refrain from lecturing piously about the virtues of humanity and accessibility. Just state your case, shrug your shoulders, smile, and leave them wondering why they never thought of it before. You'll be surprised. Once you open the gate and remove the stigma of crossing over from one camp to the other, people will follow your lead.

Step Down to Step Up

Leadership in today's emergency services means supporting an organization from the bottom of the organization chart, deep in the trenches. It's a hands-on job that requires a human touch. The result of revealing the authentic human being who's in charge of the team is that you're suddenly in a position to seek the advice and tap the experience of people around you who will surprise you with what they can contribute to the collective wisdom of the organization. You don't know it all. And everyone around you knows that you don't know it all. Pretending that you have all the answers is a dangerous practice. If the organization can move forward only on the basis of your limited knowledge and information, then it will get only as far as you are able to take it alone. Your limits will put people at risk, weaken the strength of your authority, and worst of all, block any opportunity that you might have to get more information.

I have a wise friend with a high school diploma who hired a secretary with a doctorate degree. When someone asked him if it was threatening or intimidating to have such an educated person in his employ, he just laughed. He said, "Are you kidding? I only hire people who are better and smarter than I am. They make me look good!" The point is that it's smart to surround yourself with the brightest and best, and then do everything in your power to make sure they can perform to the highest standards and assist you in pressing your organization's mission forward. Collectively, decisions will have more depth. Directions will be more clear. People will be more effective. The work will be much stronger. Effective leadership begins with you. Step down to step up.

PERSONAL STUDY EXERCISES

1. *Make a list of at least ten unspoken rules for conversation between people of different ranks.* What are the consequences of disobeying these rules? How have these rules governed how you interact with your boss?

2. *How do you know you rank above some people?* What cues do you use to demonstrate your rank? Make a list of such things as uniforms, badges, sleeping assignments, seniority when scheduling vacations, etc. Which of these things identify you as a leader? Which mark you as a manager? How can you get more of these things into the "leader" category?

3. *Identify an experience you've had where someone who outranked you needed your help and you offered it without hesitating. What happened?* What was it about that person that made you feel safe enough to offer your help? What was the reaction of the person you helped? What was the reaction of your peers? How has your relationship with the person you helped changed? Now, identify an experience where someone who outranked you needed your help and you hesitated. What happened? What was it about that person that made you reluctant to offer? How might things have been different if you had not hesitated?

CHAPTER 7

Listening

"Speak little. Do much."

—Ben Franklin

A scuba-diving friend once asked me if firefighters on a fire scene have a universal "unspoken" language that can be understood without benefit of speech or hearing—like the system of hand signals used for communicating underwater. For example, he explained, divers know that sawing your index finger once across your throat means "I am out of air." Pointing to the surface means "I am going up now." The hand signals are taught in all diving certification programs and are universally understood. When I thought about it, I realized that fire and emergency medical services don't have a comparable universal communication system. But perhaps there's no need, because the very nature of our profession requires that we master the ability to assess a situation without being told what's going on. We work where it's dark and loud, where people can't talk or listen, and yet where the need to be understood is critical. I remember being in a dark, smoke-filled building trying to locate a fellow firefighter. I tapped three times on my air tank, held my breath for a second, and strained to listen. Beyond the darkness and above the deafening din of firefighting, I heard three mimicking taps. I had asked a question. He had answered. Like dolphins using echo-location, we tapped as we moved toward each other, following each other's signals.

Unfortunately, our ability to communicate clearly breaks down when language is involved. Perhaps it's because the concepts we try to convey with language are more complicated than "Where are you?" (tap, tap, tap) and "I'm here" (tap, tap, tap). Maybe we are confused by words and body language that send mixed signals. Or perhaps it's because we aren't nearly as good at conversation as we are at tapping. The root of the problem is easily summed up by our term for "conversation." We call it "talking." We say, "John and I were just talking about that" or "We have a problem here. Let's talk about it." Interestingly, we seldom acknowledge that conversation is in fact comprised of two components: talking *and* listening. Frankly, the listening aspect of conversation is by far the more useful. Indeed, it's only when you listen that you gather information on situations and insight into people. Listening skills, although invaluable, are often overlooked in the training of a manager or the development of a leader.

Pete de Lisser of the International Listening Association reports that "it is not surprising that 75 percent of executives have been trained in speaking skills, while five percent have taken a skill course in listening. Our business experience is 'whoever draws the first breath is declared the listener.' "

If you're like most of us, as a person speaks to you, you instantaneously launch a three-part information-intake program. First, you hear the words. Second, you filter and edit them through your own experience and frames of reference. And third, you concoct an appropriate response that you can volley within a split second of your companion's silence. Your compulsion to respond is so urgent that you will punctuate your listening with facial expressions, nodding, and mumbling encouragement to continue—"right, yep, uh-huh, tsk"—in the minuscule gaps between phrases. Stephen Covey, author of *Seven Habits of Highly Effective People,* says that we listen "with the intent to reply." Communication is like a rapid ping-pong game where we expect to be able to keep the ball in play at all times. No one likes a kill shot. Silence may be golden, but it can also be intensely uncomfortable, especially if you don't know how to use it.

Listening Is Active

When we think of conversation in terms of a ping-pong game—my shot, your shot, my shot, your shot—it's easy to think of communicating as taking turns. When the other person is talking, you appear to be passive. Apparently, it's not your turn yet. When your companion stops talking, it's a signal that *now* it's your turn to talk. But "taking turns" is an illusion. When you're listening, it's more *your* turn than when you are talking. The listening phase of the process is where you get all your information. Communicating requires active involvement throughout the exchange, whether or not your mouth is open.

Exactly How Good Is a Good Listener?

Even the best of us are not very good at listening. Doubt it? Recruit the most attentive listener you know to help you conduct a little experiment that was published by Allison Schumer in the *1996 Listening Post*. Here are a few questions to ask, the responses to which may surprise you. Keep the exercise moving at a rapid clip. Under no circumstances should you stand up in your chair and shout "Wrong!" at the end of each response (although the urge will be overwhelming).

You: How many of each animal did Moses put on the Ark?
Your (really good) listener: Two.
You: No, that was Noah. Moses didn't put any animals on the Ark.

You: Spell "pop."
Your (pretty good) listener: P-O-P.
You: Spell "top."
Your (pretty good) listener: T-O-P.
You: Spell "mop."
Your (pretty good) listener: M-O-P.
You: What are you supposed to do at a green light?
Your (good) listener: Stop.
You: No, at a green light, you go.

You: Spell "host."
Your (apparently not very good) Listener: H-O-S-T.
You: Spell "most."
Your (apparently not very good) Listener: M-O-S-T.
You: What do you put in a toaster?
Your (obviously terrible) listener: Toast.
You: No, you put bread in and take toast out.

So, what's happening here? Very simply, your listener automatically did what we all do. Even as you were asking a question, he launched the three-part information-intake program we use in conversation: heard the words, filtered and edited them, and concocted an appropriate response. You hadn't even completed the question before your listener was ready to volley the reply. This is typical. Before you get self-righteous, be advised that you would have made the same mistakes. So would I. Even in a test with short, easy questions and answers, when the very ability to listen is at issue, few are able to turn off the internal monologues that we all use to make sense of "talking." Our filters are clogged. Our editors are overloaded and inaccurate. We are far too concerned with the rapid volley. But it doesn't seem to matter. Remember, we listen with the intent to reply. When our turn to talk is coming up, we have to be ready to respond, even if it's wrong.

How Do We Learn to Listen?
You're probably already a good listener. But to be a great listener, you need to practice two simple principles:

1. *Be quiet—inside and out.* Close your mouth and open your mind. First, be silent so that your companion can speak. Then, silence your mind. When listening, your single objective is to absorb information. If the information is to be accurate, you need to keep it in the form in which you accept it, without reworking it to suit you. Stop interpreting and translating—just take it in. For practice, the next time you converse with someone, be aware of the continuous monologue that is blaring in your head as the person speaks. You'll discover nonstop scripts such as "Is he kidding?" "I did that once." "Bette has one just like that." "I don't think so." " I know that can't be true." As you become aware of your interference with the information, silence the monologue until the only sound in your head is the sound of the other person's voice.

2. *Focus on the present.* Settle down and pay attention. Be in the moment. In our usual zeal to move conversation forward, we push the conversation to conclusion in a sort of linear fashion: We

greet, state the agenda, explore options, resolve issues, come to consensus (hopefully), and finish. Skilled listening doesn't demand forward advancement or conclusion. It is practiced in the present moment without regard to progressive steps. When you don't pressure, you allow a speaker to take you where he wants you to go, to say what he wants to say. You suspend time. Here's an example:

Linear Conversation Script:
  John: My dog is missing.
  Terry: Have you put up posters?
  John: Yes, and I've called the police and gone door-to-door
            in my neighborhood.
  Terry: You could call the pound.
  John: I did.

John didn't ask for Terry's help. He is telling Terry only that his dog is missing. Terry assumes that he is supposed to come up with ways to fix the situation and instantly matches John's actions against strategies that he thinks could be effective. He moves the conversation forward toward a logical conclusion, where John will finally accept a suggestion, close the encounter, and leave to do what Terry says. The conversation is decidedly linear. But that's not what John wants. Let's try it again.

Active Listening Script:
  John: My dog is missing.
  Terry: You look worried.
  John: I am. I've done everything I can think to do, but I'm
          really worried.

John is a capable man who has taken action to find his dog. He doesn't need Terry's input. What he does need, however, is support. The statement "You look worried" is the cue that the conversation is in the moment. It doesn't serve to move the conversation to conclusion. It's merely an observation that demonstrates Terry's attention to the situation and opens an opportunity to John to express himself. John talks and Terry actively listens.

The FBI Takes Active
Listening One Step Further

The science of active listening has been researched and developed for Federal Bureau of Investigation (FBI) negotiators who use finely tuned communication skills to diffuse potentially life-threatening situations. Clearly, you don't want to have *any* misunderstanding with a hostage-holding, bomb-building, bazooka-toting maniac. Of course, negotiators take active listening to its limits. Unlike most of us in conversation, an actively listening negotiator gathers information with the intent to use it to maneuver a person into making a decision that is intelligent. So, in one sense, the script of a negotiation will be linear; it will have a conclusion. But an FBI negotiator doesn't "talk" a person into seeing his point of view. He listens for cues and then manipulates them. In fact, the FBI points out that one interesting side effect of entering into a negotiation (or a conversation) as an active listener is that the person with whom you are conversing tends to listen more carefully to himself. When the pace of the conversation is slowed down by being in the present and made active, the person senses empathy, feels less threatened, and is more able to assess positions and solve problems. Although you'll likely not have to soothe the jangled nerves of a terrorist or talk a person out of jumping off a bridge, you will find the FBI negotiators' techniques useful when you're trying to be persuasive.

Offer verbal and nonverbal encouragement cues as the person speaks. You can assure the person that you are listening by focusing your attention. Make and keep eye contact, but don't stare. Be aware that researchers report that five to seven seconds is the limit for eye-to-eye contact without making the other person uncomfortable. Blinking or refocusing your eyes on something else for a split second will relax the pressure your subject may feel from an intense encounter. Let the person know that you are following his words by nodding occasionally and offering brief, well-timed verbal cues such as "I see."

Paraphrase what you've heard. When you repeat in your own words what your subject says, you accomplish one of two things. You demonstrate that you've heard him and understand the message. Or, you make clear that you have a sincere desire to understand when you give him the opportunity to confirm that you have understood correctly. Either way, your subject will be assured that you are actively listening. Be careful that you don't overdo this. Repeating every sentence is guaranteed to annoy your subject and make you sound like someone who doesn't understand a thing except the principle of killing time. Also, it's easy to sound like you're mocking the subject by playing back his words. Use this technique only on sentences that make points. Avoid beginning your paraphrase with, 'What I hear you saying is ....'" To most people, this is like fingernails on a chalkboard. To illustrate a good paraphrase, your subject says, "I didn't repack the kit because I thought Joan was going to do it. I never know when she's going to come through, and it makes me look bad." You reply, "You thought Joan was going to repack the kit, so you didn't do it. It's difficult to count on her and you think she's making you look bad." To be honest, you may or may not have gotten the point. If you did, your subject will be pleased that you understood. If you didn't, your subject will clarify the statements so that you have a better shot at understanding. Either way, you win.

Quickly reflect the thought. If FBI negotiators are unsure about how to lead a conversation with a subject, they merely repeat the last words of the subject's sentence or develop a quick, brief paraphrase of the main thought. You can do the same. For example, if your subject says, "Joan and her slovenly ways are making me crazy," you could reply, "Driving you nuts, right?" This quick feedback assures your subject that you're listening and willing to follow the conversation wherever it may lead, but you're not directing it with questions that could be interpreted as manipulative. You're able to buy time to gather information without having to take control—yet.

Acknowledge emotion without judgment. FBI negotiators learn that people define themselves and make decisions based on a set of beliefs they develop over their lifetimes. Anything that challenges those beliefs threatens their very being and, of course, triggers a stubborn defense. When you're in conversation with a person, active listening—without challenge—presents an opportunity to gently maneuver a person into accepting another point of view within his own belief system rather than your having to issue an edict. An effective tool in conversation is to acknowledge that you understand how a person feels. (You don't have to agree!) It demonstrates your attention to what is being said. Because you are bringing active listening into the conversation, you are encouraging your subject to slow down and examine his own emotional state and its relationship to the situation at hand. You could say, "It sounds like you're really ticked at Joan and blame her for not repacking the kit." Because the subject is being given the time and space to be personally reflective and is feeling safe about expressing himself, he might say, "Yeah. I'd like to slam dunk Joan into the fountain. But the truth is that repacking the kit was my responsibility. I'm more angry with myself. I should have checked with her. I'll do that next time." The truth is told. And you get insight into his feelings and plans to keep the situation from happening in the future.

Ask questions that can be answered in full sentences. When you ask a good question, you generally get a good answer. And a good answer is one that gives you information. You want your question to be answered by a moment of consideration followed by complete sentences. Examples are "What made you think that Joan would repack the kit?" and "What else has Joan done to drive you nuts?" By the way, when developing good questions, take a cue from parents who are driven to madness by the incessant queries of two-year-olds. Avoid asking "Why?" The answer will be "Because." Bad questions beget bad answers.

Get personal. When you're dealing with a person and you want him to trust you, you have to be real. The best way is to let him know you a little. FBI negotiators advise using "I" messages. For example, you might say, "I know how you feel about Joan. I'd be frustrated, too." Empathy and acknowledgment that you're "in this together" are good ways to break down barriers and build trust. But be careful to use this technique judiciously. Don't get carried away and start talking about yourself and your point of view. You'll stop listening. (And probably so will your subject!)

Sit in silence. Because most of us see conversation as a ping-pong game where it's important to keep the ball in play at all times, we dread a silence. Understanding this very human foible gives you a powerful tool in the art of conversation. Here's how it works. If you merely switch off, your subject will rush to fill the void. Listen and you'll get more information. By the way, by noticing how quickly your subject rushes to speak to fill the void, you can gauge how tense or uncomfortable he is. The faster people rush to speak, the more queasy they are about the lapse of silence. Also, you can use a well-placed silence to diffuse a hot-tempered situation. Frankly, it's hard for your subject to keep yelling at you if you don't yell back. Remember that your ability to practice active listening gently leads your subject into actively listening to himself. Likely he'll resolve his own anger without your having to say a word. To give you an example, your subject yells, "That Joan! She wants me to look bad! And she has you snowed into thinking that she can do no wrong!" You sit and wait. He can't stand the silence and continues: "You aren't snowed, are you?" You sit and wait. He continues: "OK, she isn't out to ruin my reputation, but I'm still miffed." There. He said it. The situation is resolved.

Using Your Listening Ability for More Than Words

Researchers report that we speak approximately 175 words a minute, but we can listen to and process about 400. What do we do with this "surplus" of listening ability? We need to invest it in observing and interpreting nonverbal cues. The truth is that we get nearly 93 percent of our information from nonverbal communication, those other signals besides the spoken language that we use to communicate. I have a friend who talks "baby talk" to her dog. You know the tone of voice. It's a high-pitched sing-song. Her dog loves it. He wags his tail and nearly turns himself inside out with delight. One day I remarked that her dog really enjoyed being praised and seemed to understand perfectly how wonderful she thought he was. She laughed and said, "He has no clue what I'm saying. He only understands my tone of voice. Watch this." She then used the same tone of voice but instead of crooning "Good dog, good boy, smart puppy," she substituted "When did you get to be such a moron? You're too stupid to live. I want a cat." The dog was totally delighted and my friend made her point.

Besides tone of voice, we also use "body language"—the ways we express ourselves with postures and gestures in our bodies. Some of the messages we control. And some are so much a part of human nature that we aren't aware that we're making ourselves understood loud and clear without a word. The easiest body language to study is facial expression. Researchers have discovered that even newborn infants clearly understand the most subtle expressions. Smile means happy. Frown means angry. You know the range. Take a moment to refresh your memory by reading the following short list and express each thought with your face and a slight head movement:

I'm happy.
I'm sad.
I'm angry.
I'm enraged.
I'm afraid.
I'm surprised.
I'm confused.
I like you.
I love you.
I dislike you.
I hate you.
I agree with you.
I think you're out of your mind.

The actual list is practically endless, but you get the point. Facial expressions, even if flashed for a nanosecond, can either confirm or totally contradict what a person is saying. For example, if the person says "I'm not mad" but his eyebrows are knitted together and his face is tense, you know he's fuming. Here's where mixed signals really make conversation interesting. When you pay attention, you hear words but you listen for truth. Seeing is believing.

Reading facial expressions is easy if you're observant and vigilant. Far more difficult to read are messages sent from the rest of the body. Many are so subtle that we aren't overtly aware of them in ourselves or others. Too bad. They are, in fact, the best communication tools we have. Professional actors are trained to transform themselves into characters very unlike themselves and make us believe that the fantasy they spin is the truth. First they memorize a script. Mere words. That's the easy part. Any one of us could do the same, although few of us could transform the words into a believable scenario. The thing that professional actors do to make us believe that their characters are real is to control their bodies—

their nonverbal communication. One of the first training exercises they master is the suppression of evidence of fear. It's called "getting the creature under control." Acting coaches know that stage fright is a very real impediment to performing. Therefore, it's the first emotion to be tackled. You've heard the expression "Never let them see you sweat." It comes from actors who know they have to deceive an audience into thinking that they're comfortable. The first step in fear suppression is to acknowledge that fear *shows* itself somewhere in the body. The actor does a methodical body scan to identify its manifestation—the "creature." A dry mouth. A shaking knee. A clenched fist. Rocking. A tight throat. Once he locates the creature, his job is to banish it with a variety of techniques. Mastering fear gives the actor the first measure of control over his body and is the beginning of a whole bag of tricks that he uses to give the illusion of truth to his words.

Fortunately for us, few people are going to have the training and skill of a professional actor. Because most people aren't even aware that the creature or any of its cousins exist, much less have the skill to get them under control, they are open books for active listeners who are observant. With practice and patience, you can learn to attune to body language in yourself and others.

A Vocabulary Lesson in Body Language

The body has a lot to say if you learn how to listen. Here's a list of some of its secret vocabulary:

Rocking, bobbing, or bouncing: "I'm tense, nervous, or uncomfortable."

Clenched fists: "I'm holding back" or "I'm angry."

Index finger raised slightly: "I want to speak now or interrupt you" or "Warning!"

Hands limp or hanging: "I'm bored or restless. Get on with it."

Touching hair: "I'm really uncomfortable here."

Touching hair while making intense eye contact: "I find you attractive."

Fiddling or twiddling with hands and fingers: "I'm nervous or uncomfortable."

Scratching or stroking: "I'm nervous or uncomfortable."

Jiggling or swinging a foot: "I'm nervous or uncomfortable."

Leaning toward you: "I agree with you totally."

Leaning away from you: "I disagree. You're out of your mind."

Clearing throat: "I am struggling to get under control."

Voice constricted: "I'm afraid."

Licking or pressing lips together: "I'm nervous or uncomfortable."

Laughing too loudly: "I am really tense, but I don't want you to realize it."

Stiffening: "I'm lying."

Sitting very still while speaking: "I'm lying."

Hesitating before speaking: "I'm getting ready to lie and have to construct it carefully."

Folding arms: "I feel defensive and attacked. I've got to protect myself."

Crossing legs: "I feel defensive and attacked. I've got to protect myself."

Turning away from you: "I feel defensive and attacked. I've got to break contact with you."

Making eye contact: "I'm listening. I'm here."

Looking down: "I feel rejected."

Avoiding eye contact: "I don't feel secure or included here."

Looking up when talking about the past: "I mean what I say."

Looking side to side when talking about the present: "I mean what I say."

Eyes constantly moving upward when talking about the present: "I've memorized what I'm telling you. It's rehearsed."

Eyes move side to side when talking about the past or recalling information: "I'm lying."

Eyes never move up when recalling information: "I'm lying."

Staring: "I dislike you intensely."

Dr. Albert E. Scheflin, who studies group interaction, noticed a peculiar phenomenon in discussion groups. When the group agrees with the speaker, they all assume his position. If he shifts position, everyone in the group will shift positions to match his. How can you use this information? You'll know that a person agrees with you when that person changes position to stand or sit as you are. Confirm your agreement by changing positions and notice that the person follows your lead. Another fun exercise is to enter a meeting and ferret out people who are uncomfortable by scratching the back of your hand for a minute. Everyone who is uncomfortable will do the same. Psychologists call this unconscious mimicking behavior the "dance of synchrony." We all dance with each other constantly. Knowing how to follow and lead makes you a better dancer.

How to Get People to Listen to You

The day will come when you need to talk and get someone else to listen and understand clearly. You now know the bad news, that very few people are good listeners. So how do you command the attention of the inattentive? How do you improve the odds that you will be understood? Here are a few basic suggestions:

Converse in a setting with as few distractions as possible.

Sit or stand straight. Good posture is perceived as commanding power.

Relax.

Look directly at the person.

Before you speak, organize your thoughts.

Be concise and direct.

Remember to listen actively to the response you get.

Sorting Through the Input

As an active listener, you'll receive a great deal of information, some good and some not so good. How do you sort through the possibilities and select the useful? Communications experts recommend that you learn to evaluate information. Here are four tips for evaluating:

1. *The first thing you heard wasn't necessarily the best thing you heard.* There is a very human tendency to give credence to the first thing you heard, even though the real truth might be buried in the second, third, and fourth things you heard. (By the way, here's another way to use this information. If you want to influence someone

unskilled at active listening to do things your way, be first in line to deliver information.)

2. *Always listening to the same people and giving their opinions more weight will narrow your possibilities for hearing truth.* Good leaders are smart enough to widen their circles of influence. You never know when you will be surprised by a person who comes out of left field and delivers a stunning revelation. You'll miss it if you discount everyone outside your inner circle.

3. *Focus on positive information and resist the urge to let negatives dominate your decisions.* Interestingly, when human beings process information, we focus on negative information. If you consider two facts side by side, one positive and one negative, you'll determine that the negative one is more important and you'll be able to recall it long after the positive fact has slipped out of your database. It's true. When you're a practiced listener, you have to take this human peculiarity into consideration and evaluate both sides of an issue, giving equal consideration to them.

4. *Information should be stored, no matter how irrelevant it might seem at the time you receive it.* Leadership requires innovation—that knack for combining unusual bits of seemingly unrelated information into something new and creative. If you don't have a wide assortment of ideas to combine, you can't come up with innovative ideas. It's important that you pay attention to the world and collect ideas as you go along. You never know when it will come in handy; when it will click with something else and suddenly, surprisingly transform into something remarkable.

The Training Advantage of Emergency Services

Fortunately, emergency services personnel have a good start at being good listeners. We're trained to take in information from a variety of sources—verbal and nonverbal—simultaneously. Interestingly, this "intake" skill and its translation into leadership ability were first studied in physicians who made the transition from clinical practice into medical administration. Researchers discovered that physicians have a unique ability to "read" patients. Here's how it works in the clinic. To make a diagnosis, the clinician conducts an interview. He asks the question, "What seems to be the trouble here?" Listening carefully, the physician is searching for other verbal cues such as ability to articulate, cadence of speech, or appropriateness of content. In addition, the physician is acutely aware of nonverbal cues such as body language and general appearance. Combining the information from multiple cues, the physician is able to move closer to an accurate assessment. For example, if the patient says "I'm fine" but is pale, sweating, and protecting his left side, the physician may conclude that the patient is stoic and yet in pain. At this point, the physician may seek clarification or more information. Again, he will take in information on several levels simultaneously and will employ the acumen and analytical ability that are the signatures of effective medical personnel. The entire process begins with listening to what is said and not said, and how. This ability to read a person is an invaluable tool when it's translated into leadership. You already have it.

Leadership in Emergency Services
Requires Listening Without Retribution

When the South Canyon fire swept up Storm King Mountain in Colorado on July 6, 1994, 14 firefighters died. Yet the nightmare was far from over. By the end of the year, wildfires had claimed 34 lives, destroyed millions of acres of land, and cost nearly one billion dollars. Without question, 1994 was one of the most devastating years for firefighting in this century. But in all that was lost, something was gained. Sweeping reforms—all targeted at safety—focused the firefighting industry's attention on protecting its personnel. The seeds for reform were planted in the hours following Storm King Mountain, when a joint Bureau of Land Management/ U.S. Forest Service investigation team was engaged to investigate what went horribly wrong. When they filed their reports, Land Management and the Forest Service established the Interagency Management Review Team (IMRT) to study the investigation team's findings, review their recommendations, and propose a plan for corrective action. No one wanted to see a repeat performance of Storm King Mountain—*ever.* By October 1994, their conclusions and recommendations were presented to and accepted by five wild-land fire agencies and by senior safety and health officials of the two departments involved. Of course, the report is comprehensive and covers a great many key issues. Among them is the issue of two-way communication without retribution.

For the first time, firefighters were being given the mandated authority to express opinions regarding safety to superior officers without damaging consequences, and superior officers were ordered to listen.

The Need for Trust

Without question, trusting your own judgment and being able to express your opinions are critical when your personal safety is at stake. As a leader, you also have to be willing to listen to and hear what other people have to say to you. In an interesting study of the captains of aircraft crews, investigators found that the best captains acknowledged that their ability to make decisions in emergencies was not as good as it was in calmer moments. So, when the chips were down, those good captains turned to others for input and advice. On the other hand, captains who ranked as poor reported that they were equally skilled in both emergencies and calm moments. They thought they had all the answers. Of course, this is precisely why they were ranked "poor" captains. They never asked for help or accepted suggestions. The problem is that a nonlistener might operate with misinformation but is unwilling to let it go, even when it fails to yield good results. A threatened person has to protect the fragile illusion of being right. Great leadership requires the mouth to close and the mind to open. Only by active listening will you be able to get expanded information and other points of view from the rich experience of the people around you. Only then will you be a leader.

Communication Is a Two-Way Street With No Back Alleys

As a good leader, you need feedback. You need to know how things are going, how your people are doing, and how you're doing. If you rely on normal channels, you'll wait forever. One of the old-est axioms in organizational communication is that more information trickles down than seeps up. The military calls this phenomenon "stovepipe communication," meaning that information flows only vertically (mostly down) in the organization. The military actively discourages restricted communication, knowing that it can be deadly in battle conditions. They train their troops to rely on horizontal communication as well—information that comes from neither above nor below but from someone beside you. Formally, you might be passed information that you need by someone appointed to tell you. Informally, you might hear information through the grapevine. Unfortunately, the higher up you are, the fewer people there are beside you and the shorter your grapevine (if you have one at all). It's true. So how do you get information that provides you with great feedback if your communication conduit is inadequate? Simple. You build a better conduit. First, you have to create a culture in your organization that allows everyone to feel safe. As the IMRT recommends, people need to be able to talk to you without fear of retribution. They have to be able to tell you things without your flying off the handle or holding grudges. And you have to respect the power of two heads being better than one when you're struggling with a decision. Other people and their points of view have to factor into your work. Every good decision starts with evaluation. You can't know what to do next if you don't know what's going on now, and you need all the information you can get. The way to get that information is by active listening.

PERSONAL STUDY EXERCISES

1. Use active listening in a casual conversation. Suspend time. Merely listen and respond without trying to bring the conversation to conclusion.

2. Pay attention to body language in a conversation that you can't hear. For instance, observe a conversation at a table across a crowded restaurant. Create a script without hearing a word.

3. When you're engaged in intense discussion with someone, change your position and observe whether or not your companion signals his agreement with you by following your lead.

CHAPTER 8

Motivating People

"If you'd have a servant that you like, serve your self."
—Ben Franklin

Because the very nature of leadership requires you to accomplish your mission by way of the efforts and cooperation of other people, you have to know how to motivate them. They have to want to work with you, even with the worst assignments under the toughest conditions in the world. Few people can understand our profession, and even fewer can understand why we love it so much. If they knew that, they would know why we're here.

Help Wanted

Men and women to work 24-hour shifts. Must be able to drive huge vehicles at breakneck speed through snarled traffic; climb up and down wet ladders; enter burning buildings; put out fires; carry other full-sized adults; administer skilled medical attention under impossible field conditions; prepare meals three times a day for groups of ten or more (only half of whom will approve of the choice of menu); fill out endless reports; and maintain vehicles, tools, and equipment for peak performance at all times. Must be able to follow orders without question, think and act independently, and unfailingly know how to reconcile these two opposing directives. Attractive uniform provided (weighs approximately 85 pounds). No sleep required and little allowed. Must work well with others, including coworkers, administrators, arsonists, drunks, psychopaths, and the general public.

A friend of mine, who is the human resources director for an accounting firm, laughs at my help wanted ad. She chides, "Mike, this ad for fire-rescue personnel is hysterical. But if you ever dare to place it, you won't get a single person to apply!" I beg to differ. I know something that she doesn't know—that some people are born to be in emergency services. You know who you are. This profession, in spite of all of its difficulties and inconveniences, beckons you with the seductive lure of a siren's song. Emergency services has been called a "passion with a paycheck."

In many traditional corporate work settings, money is considered to be the prime motivator. It's certainly the easiest. Historically, annual increases, incentive raises, and performance bonuses line the pockets of workers who stay long and do well. But research clearly demonstrates that it takes more than mere cash to give a person the extra spark he needs to give 110 percent to the job. Emergency services, where salaries and raises are tightly controlled and capped, can't rely at all on money to motivate employees. The question then is, How do we motivate?

Knowing how to motivate a person in emergency services requires that you understand the person, the passion, and the paycheck. In *that* order.

The Real Yet Secret Reasons People Work

The 1993 National Study of the Changing Workforce reveals startling truths about what motivates employees. When employees were asked the reasons considered to have been "very important" in deciding to take a job with a current employer, the top variable listed by 65 percent of the respondents was "open communication," followed by "effect on personal/family life," "nature of work," and "management quality." "Wages" ranked 16th on the list, just two places ahead of "didn't receive any other job offers."

Researchers have identified several core characteristics that make a job attractive. *Inc.* magazine conducted a survey of U.S. workers to determine what factors bear on employee satisfaction and job performance. The factors are:

The opportunity to do every day what they do best.

A supervisor or a colleague who cares about them.

Their opinions are listened to and taken into account.

The job offers opportunities for growth and learning.

The mission of the employer makes the employees feel that their jobs are important.

They have the materials, equipment, and information to do the job right.

Did you notice that "high salary" doesn't appear on the list? Does that surprise you? It shouldn't. Money ranks fairly low on most employees' wish lists.

The difference between a motivating incentive like "opportunity to do every day what they do best" and mere money is that money is an entitlement. If you were to draw up an employee's bill of rights, money would certainly head the list. Entitlements are givens. They comprise the checklist of items that every employee expects as baseline requirements of the job. Your employee entitlements are:

A fair wage for the job.

Safe working conditions.

Tools and equipment.

Uniforms.

Policies, procedures, and administration.

Never mistake an entitlement as an incentive to work.

Motivation Starts When You Hire the Right People

Human resources experts tell us that if you want a person to perform, you have to hire the right person. Author Frederick Herzberg says, "If you want people to be motivated to do a good job, then give them a good job to do." Your job as the leader is to hire the right people, give them the right tools, and then let them do their jobs. No amount of motivation in the world will make a successful neurosurgeon out of a chef. You can't offer that chef anything that will suddenly inspire him to exhibit the skill of a physician. You'll discourage the chef if you have him believing that neurosurgery is possible. He'll feel like a failure. Additionally, the fact that he'll disappoint you will be crushing.

It's important to place the right people in the right jobs. They have to be able to do whatever it is you need done. If you hire an overly qualified person, that employee will be bored and insulted. If you hire an underqualified person, that employee will go insane trying to deal with failure after failure.

Studies show that when you hire skillfully and do a good job of matching the person to the position, good things happen.

Those employees expect things, in general, to work out well. When employees expect that all will go well, they approach their duties with confidence and enthusiasm.

They expect their best efforts to be successful. When things go wrong, as they might, those employees will view the incident as a temporary setback. After all, this is supposed to work! They'll be more resourceful and creative in finding ways to achieve.

They see potentials rather than roadblocks. There's an unmistakable confidence that accompanies the expectation of success. Employees who have it aren't discouraged by delays in their progress. They merely drop back and punt. They might even see the problems as welcome challenges.

Bob Nelson, vice president of Blanchard Training and Development, says, "The leader's job is to work with the employee to mesh individual needs and interests such as career aspirations and learning goals with the organization's needs for performance and results. Effective leadership is what you do with employees, not what you do to them." Never mistake the value of your people!

A very wise officer once said, "Our company's most valuable assets go home every night."

Owning the Mission

Frankly, the old command-and-control method to motivate employees no longer works. Our workplaces have evolved beyond the time when orders were barked and obeyed without question. Today, employees are far more sophisticated. Fortunately, so is our ability to create professional environments where everyone has a place in the organization and a stake in the outcome of the work. The secret is in *ownership*.

You now know that leadership is a matter of consensus. You and the people who follow you all have to be in agreement on key issues. They have to think as you think, share your values, and understand the mission as you understand it. When you're "all in this together," the mission no longer belongs to you alone. "You" have just become "we." Your mission becomes the mission of the group. You all own it together. One of the often-cited experts in employee ownership is a U.S. Air Force lieutenant general who for many years headed the U.S. Strategic Air Command. He was the military version of a CEO and president. He received many citations for his leadership skills in creating a workforce that "owned" the Strategic Air Command, embraced its mission as a team, and behaved accordingly. Those people weren't really employee owners—or were they? Although it's impossible to own SAC, they *did* in fact own their employer's mission—they were united in their values and their vision.

Experts use this general as a stellar example of a leader who recognized the importance of culture. His methods were based largely on trust and good communication within his team. They knew what he expected from them. He knew what they expected from him. They all worked on their mission together.

Your job, as a leader, is to bring the mission to your people and share it with them. When you all own it, you all serve it.

The Effective Motivator

To be an effective motivator, you have to ask four key questions:

1. What is it that I am asking this person to do?
2. Why would this person not want to do this?
3. Why would this person want to do this?
4. Am I willing and able to make this task one that the person will undertake?

The characteristics of a good motivator include:

Credibility. You have to be sincere and believable.
Competence. You have to know what you're talking about and understand what you're asking.

Capability. You have know enough about what you're asking to be able to make the situation safe and the expectations realistic.

Control. You have to have a grasp of the situation and be able to create an environment or circumstance that is safe for the employee.

Confidence. You have to trust your employee's judgment and skill.

The Value of Positive Feedback

The undeniable superiority of positive feedback is cleverly demonstrated in an exercise developed by world-renowned biologist and author Dr. John Paling. Working with an audience, he sends one person out of the room. Then he hides a prize somewhere among the remaining audience members, who are told that, when the absent person returns, they're to assist the person in finding the prize by shouting encouragement: "Carrot! Carrot! Carrot!" when the person is getting close to it. When the absent person reenters the room, John instructs him or her to find the prize and says that the audience will help. Merry chaos ensues, of course, and the person finds the prize rather quickly. Then John sends another person out of the room and hides another prize. This time, however, he tells the audience that they're to help the person find the prize by shouting discouragement: "Stick! Stick! Stick!" when the person moves away from the prize. They're to let the person know that the selected direction is wrong. When the absent person reenters the room, John instructs him or her to find the prize and explains how the audience will help. This time, the chaos is not merry. It gets pretty tense, and something very interesting happens every time: The person can't find the prize as quickly.

The principles are dramatic and simple. With positive feedback, a person feels encouraged, certain that the chosen course is the right one, and he enjoys the praise and camaraderie of being helped by the audience. With negative feedback, the person knows only that he is going the wrong way. Not only must the person deflect critical shouting, but he must also make an adjustment in the chosen course without being certain that even the new direction will be a right one. When the new choice is greeted with negative feedback, the person grows anxious. Confidence drops, humiliation sets in, and the person's ability to make decisions is compromised by an overriding need to self-protect. Additionally, the opportunity to shout negative feedback gives some audience members license to become aggressive.

If John were to take the experiment one step further and arrange for "Carrot!" and "Stick!" to be shouted an equal number of times, you could be certain that the person trying to find the prize would listen almost exclusively to the "Carrot" shouters. If you were to ask later which word had been used more frequently, he would tell you "Carrot."

After examining and asking employees about 65 potential incentives in the workplace, Dr. Gerald Graham of Wichita State University found the top five motivating incentives were initiated by managers and based on employee performance:

- Manager personally congratulates employees who do a good job.
- Manager writes personal notes for good performance.
- Organization uses performance as the major basis for promotion.
- Manager publicly recognizes good performance.
- Manager holds morale-building meetings to celebrate success.

Positive reinforcement is far more valuable and effective than negative feedback. A word of encouragement goes a very long way for both the giver and the receiver.

When you decide that it's the right thing to do:

- Write a letter to the employee.
- Write a letter to the employee's family.
- Say thank you.
- Give more responsibility.
- Seek advice from the employee.
- Issue a commendation.
- Recommend a raise.
- Give good performance evaluations.
- Enter a note in the logbook.

Be specific in your positive feedback. Say what the employee did and why it was valuable to you. Simple gestures indicate that you are not too busy to miss noticing that an employee has done something special.

Motivating People Through Their Value Systems

Dr. Layne Longfellow, a psychologist who works with human resources, reports: "You don't motivate people though your value system, you motivate people through their own value system. You don't manage or sell to people through your value system, you manage and sell to them through their own value system. You don't govern and educate people through your own value system, you govern and educate them through theirs."

Times are changing and so are the people who grow up in them! In 1924, American parents were surveyed on the character traits that they would most like their children to develop. The answers were: (1) strict obedience and (2) loyalty to traditional institutions.

By 1988, the world had changed radically. The Institute for Survey Research at the University of Michigan asked those same questions of parents. The answers were: (1) independence and (2) tolerance of differences.

So what's the significance of two generations whose values are 180 degrees apart from each other? We have a generation reared on obedience and loyalty leading a generation reared on independence and tolerance. No wonder intergenerational communication is riddled with confusion, conflict, and collision of lifestyle and attitudes. No wonder there is a gap between trying to motivate and actually succeeding. In fact, it's a wonder that anyone ever succeeds at all!

A Look at the Generations And Their Differences

According to Longfellow, those born from 1929 to 1941 constitute the In-Charge Generation. Ninety percent of all board chairmen of the top 1000 *Fortune* companies were born before 1939. These are the Depression babies all grown up. When they were infants, their parents were trained to feed them on rigid schedules, hungry or not. Their parents were encouraged to wean them on equally rigid schedules, ready or not. The poor little tykes were to be toilet-trained by eight months, whether or not they could even sit upright on their own. Consequently,

Depression babies grew up to be unrealistic in their self-expectations, obsessed with detail, compulsive about schedules, and overly concerned with success. They are fearful of being without and are very security- and safety-oriented. Their identity is closely defined by their jobs. Who they are and what they do are one and the same.

By the early 1940s, the world was changing rapidly. Society was becoming mobile, nuclear families moved away from their extended families' homesteads, generations separated geographically, dads worked away from home, the infant mortality rate dropped, child rearing relaxed considerably, and children were given more personal freedom to explore the world and reach their own conclusions than in any other generation. Babies born during this time were in the gap between the Depression and the Baby Boom and may be able to relate to both generations on either side, even when those generations can't relate to each other. For this reason, this group is considered a bridge.

People born after World War II up until the early Sixties are the Baby Boomers, the largest generation in our history. These babies were reared by the two previous generations, who vowed that their children would never have to struggle as hard as they had and worked to assure a world of freedom and plenty. Consequently, Baby Boomers see the world as being abundant and secure. There is no apparent need to squirrel away money because it is a limitless resource. Additionally, this group is called the "Me Generation" because their parents' focus on their happiness and well-being gave them a sense of self-importance and entitlement.

The children of the Baby Boomers constitute Generation X. These are the twenty-something citizens; the first generation who can learn nothing from their grandparents because the world that their grandparents knew is gone forever. For them, finding mentors or blocks of tried-and-true information on which to build foundations is difficult. Like the Boomers, they have grown up in abundance with a high standard of living and quality education and medical care. In addition, this generation has had access to information through technology and media that exceeds any previously known in history. It is said that a 12-year-old today has had more exposure to information than Benjamin Franklin, William Shakespeare, and Abraham Lincoln had in their lifetimes combined. Not surprisingly, they feel disconnected and isolated, because what they have in information, they lack in experience.

We have all five generations in the workforce right now. Knowing that each of the five was reared differently and has different values gives you an advantage in knowing which buttons to push to motivate them. A hot button for one will leave another ice cold. For example, people born during the Depression are likely to be workaholics and very oriented toward security. If you want to offer incentive to them, you might offer a cash bonus that can be collected at the successful completion of a difficult project. They are very comfortable with the concept of hard work followed by the guarantee of a reward. Remember that such a person sees the world as unsafe and unpredictable—anything that feathers the nest or secures the future is welcomed. If you aren't in a position to offer money (and most of us in emergency services aren't), think about other things that might equate to job security—-a letter of commendation to the supervisor, a recommendation for promotion, or praise that uses verbiage such as "We can *always* count on you." Or "What did we *ever* do without you?" Time frames should be rigid and expectations should be spelled out.

But before you thank me for giving you the key to the universe, be advised that someone born during the Depression is the *only* employee who might be likely to respond to money. The same attempt at incentive might only annoy a Baby Boomer. Remember that this generation doesn't place such a high premium on money or security. They enjoy the challenge and adventure of the work more, and they value freedom.

To motivate a Baby Boomer, you might lay out the project without guidelines. In other words, tell him or her what you need to have done but refrain from giving instructions about how the job is to be completed. Because a Boomer values freedom, you might offer a vacation day in exchange for the successful completion of the project. If you are not in a position to bargain with time off, you might be surprised at the success of merely stepping back. Freedom—noninterference—during the project means that you have trust, and it feels wonderful to a Baby Boomer who prizes independence.

To motivate a Generation Xer to perform, you might be most successful by creating an alliance—literally constructing a connection for the disconnected. Assign an older partner who can help the younger employee use his or her vast storehouse of theoretical knowledge, but put it into a context where it's useful and certain to succeed. These people operate with a terrifying conundrum: They know more than anyone else and yet they aren't sure that what they know is enough. It can be unsettling. When knowledge is put to practical use, success begets success. The Postwar Pragmatist is validated, and the world becomes safer.

Because the American workforce is built on a system that was developed by people born during the Depression, who value hard work and money, three out of four U.S. corporations rely on some sort of reward incentive plan. Plaques go up on the walls. Bonuses line the pockets. Stock options. Commissions. Parking places. Kudos in the company newsletter. Halls of Fame. The list goes on. But we know that no generation past the children of the Depression places a high premium on reward incentives. A reward incentive can backfire.

How Reward Can Blow Up in Your Face

Now that you know how to reward, be careful when you use it. If you have a culture of ownership, where the mission is mutually agreed on and embraced by all of the people in your company, you won't need to reward. Some experts warn that rewarding can be a dangerous disincentive.

The reason that reward doesn't work well with most people is that punishment and reward are not really opposites. They are, in truth, two sides of the same coin. When you tell an employee "If you do well, you'll get this reward," there is a veiled underside to the statement—an implied threat of punishment. The employee might very well ask, "And what happens if I *don't* do well?" This raises the point that rewards can be damaging.

If you offer an incentive and the employee fails to produce results that earn it, then the employee feels like a failure and feels punished. Rewards are dangerous when they are offered in a competitive environment. Programs that pit individuals or teams against each other are damaging to the culture of your department. Period. A couple of years ago, a fire station staged a contest to see which shift could keep the cleanest kitchen for one week. The shift that did the best job would be treated to a barbecue by the other shifts and get a little Golden Sponge trophy. It seemed like an innocuous way to get firefighters to tidy up and have a little fun, too. But problems began almost immediately.

The contest became "us" versus "them." People took sides. Shifts began to scrutinize and criticize the efforts of the other shifts. People were singled out. Finally, as the deadline for tallying points and awarding the Golden Sponge loomed near, shifts started undermining other shifts by taking cleaning supplies and equipment home so that they wouldn't be available. When someone on a shift slipped up and committed the unpardonable sin of leaving a glass out on the counter, brother and sister firefighters turned on him. Instead of supporting each other, the firefighters were watching each other. Instead of working together, the shifts were working against each other. The results were disastrous. The winners of the Golden Sponge were accused of unfair practices, cheating, and politicking. The barbecue was canceled. It took months to untangle the mess, soothe the ruffled feathers, and restore trust.

Alfie Kohn, author of the controversial *Punished by Rewards,* makes a good point when he says that reward, like punishment, is highly effective at producing *temporary* compliance with a directive. In other words, if you tell an employee to do a job well in exchange for a day off, you'll likely get what you want. The employee will do the job well. But the motivation is misplaced and the enthusiasm is guaranteed to be short-lived. Performance outcome on that particular job is equated with the day off—not the myriad of reasons that the job should have been done well in the first place. Understanding and taking responsibility for quality work won't translate into the next job. You'll be stuck with an employee who is looking to you for reward at every juncture. Work and job performance will become halting, and you'll be in for a negotiating session with every small assignment. You'll have set up a quid pro quo relationship, where bargaining is personal between the employee and you. Instead of looking to the job for intrinsic reward—personal satisfaction—the employee will look to you. And woe be unto you the first time that the completion of a job isn't accompanied by reward. The employee will be confused, anxious, angry, and harder to motivate on the next round.

Don't think that dangling a reward will make you popular. On the contrary, your very presence and the fact that you are sitting in judgment is like having the sword of Damocles hanging by a hair over the employee's head. He or she will learn to watch for you. Worse, that employee will hide from you anything that you might perceive as being incompetent and that might jeopardize the reward. Not that the employee will make many mistakes, because there will be no risk taking, no creative thinking, and no innovation in the execution and completion of the project. Heaven knows, the employee will take no chances that could result in any kind of failure. Research confirms that the employee who works for reward will gravitate toward and prefer easy tasks. Also, the employee will develop tunnel vision and stay totally focused on the project that promises to yield reward rather than attend to any other project that isn't directly related to the task at hand, no matter how important it might be.

Offer the wrong reward, and you'll likely foster employees who are dependent, resentful, competitive, conniving, lazy, secretive, tunnel-visioned, paranoid, self-interested, insecure, and hesitant. Sounds like punishment to me. Yours and theirs.

Recent studies have revealed a startling yet logical truth. When one offers a reward for performance, the job becomes *work*. Until the moment that a misguided motivator sullies it with reward, the job might have been seen as a challenge, a personal mission, or play—it might have been fun. In one demonstration of the disincentive effects of offering a reward, a group of kids gave researchers dramatic insight. The scientists put each kid in the group into a private room with a hidden camera and gave him or her a jigsaw puzzle to assemble. Half of the kids were each given the puzzle with instructions to put it together as best they could. The consequences of success or failure or timing were not discussed. No one said, "If you do well, then we'll take you out for ice cream." Nor did anyone say, "If you fail to get this puzzle together, you'll never taste ice cream again in your life." The other half of the kids were each given the puzzle and five dollars to complete it. The kids were all given the same puzzle, so the five-dollar puzzle wasn't more difficult than the puzzle without a cash incentive. The results of the experiment were interesting. The kids who *were not* paid assembled their puzzles faster than the kids who *were*. When the kids were interviewed later, they were candid as only kids can be. The kids with money said, "It felt like work. I felt pressured. I hated it." The kids who were not offered money said, "It was a challenge. It was a game. I liked it!"

Rewarding can be interpreted as bribing. Researchers warn that changing the nature of the bribe will neither affect nor sweeten the outcome.

True Reward

All behavior is controlled by its consequences—you get what you reward. If you want creative thinking, reward creative thinking. True reward, however, comes from *being* motivated, not receiving motivation. Let me explain the difference. Being committed to your mission—*owning it*—is what motivates you to accomplish it.

PERSONAL STUDY EXERCISES

1. The next time you're in a position to work with a team of people, give them ownership of the mission by stating the objective, by asking opinions, and by letting them decide what to do and how. Your job will to be to assist and keep track of all of the components.

2. Scan your organization and identify one man or woman from each of Longfellow's generational segments. Match his theories against things you know to be true of each person you select.

3. Make a list of the reasons you're in your profession. What motivates *you?*

CHAPTER 9

Evaluating People

"A lie stands on one leg, the truth on two."

—Ben Franklin

Y ou can't lead in a vacuum. There have to be people involved. As you climb the organizational ladder in emergency services, you'll find yourself in charge of more and more employees— some directly and some indirectly. As a leader, you'll find yourself increasingly in partnership with them, relying on their efforts to get the work done. It's important to hone your people skills until you are adept at judging their strengths and weaknesses so that you can cultivate strengths and shore up weaknesses. In the workplace, we sensitively rephrase this ability to judge as "evaluating." It's the beginning of decision making about people, yourself included.

Let's Start With the Person
Closest to You: You

Performance evaluation is the responsibility of all leaders. But what happens as you climb the company ladder and there are fewer and fewer people above you on the organization chart? Who evaluates you? I have a flash for you. *You* do. And so does everyone else. Every day. They just don't tell you. Before you get up and close your door, relax. You need to know what they observe so you will have an opportunity to grow and improve. As I said, you can't know what to do next if you don't know what's going on now.

Mirror, Mirror on the Wall:
Five Ways to See Yourself

Robert Burns, the Scottish poet and a contemporary of Ben Franklin, wrote, "O wad some power the giftie gie us to see oursel's as others see us." The line is from a poem he wrote about a pretty woman sitting in church who was full of herself and her own beauty but was unaware that she had a louse (one of a family of lice!) crawling on her. Without the melodic strains of bagpipes and a rolling Highlands accent, let me translate. What Burns was saying poetically is that it would be grand to see ourselves as others see us.

There are five ways to stand back and take a good look at yourself.

1. *Take the rating sheet and have a go at it in private.* Years ago, before I applied for the mortgage for my first home, I pulled my personal credit report from the largest of the independent credit bureaus. (Credit bureaus track your financial activity monthly and make that detailed information available to people who are considering lending you money or giving you a credit card.) I knew that, the minute I filled out a mortgage application, the bank was going to pull my credit report. I wanted to see it first. First, I wanted to review it for accuracy. Second, if there was something questionable in the report, I wanted either to correct it or to be able to explain it to the potential lender. The benefits of previewing an upcoming performance evaluation are similar. But, unlike your credit report, your performance evaluation is a blank. You have to fill it out.

Conducting your own private performance evaluation is a good way to take a look at yourself within your work environment. Your organization has a standard evaluation form that lists all of the technical and personal skills they expect you to have to do your job. Even better, the evaluation form also provides some sort of measurable rating system. For example, it says something like:

Attendance: Always comes to work. (5 points)
Occasionally misses work. (4 points)
Sometimes comes to work. (3 points)
Seldom comes to work. (2 points)
We aren't sure this person still works here. (1 point)
Who? (0 points)

Either your personnel department can provide you with a blank form or you can photocopy a previous evaluation from your personal work file. If you use a copy of an old evaluation, use correction fluid to delete all of your ratings and recopy it so that you can have a clean form. But don't discard the old evaluation. Being able to compare "then" and "now" is a good way to see how far you've come, if at all.

Fill out your private performance evaluation with a pencil in hand. Vow to be brutally honest. After all, you're the only one who's going to see the results. In a quick sweep, go through the skills and assign ratings. Then, go back to each skill and rating, stop, and put it to the acid test. Ask, "Really? Am I sure? Is it possible that I'm really a little better at this than I indicated? Could it be that I'm really a little less skilled? Do I remember anything that happened this past year that could affect this rating? Has anyone said anything to me recently about my ability in this particular skill?" Adjust the ratings as you wish. Interestingly, if you lay the evaluation aside and take it again in two weeks, you might find differences in your ratings. Mood and self-esteem play important roles in your ability to see yourself. No matter what the outcome, however, you will have taken a sharp and valuable look at yourself.

2. *Stand far away from yourself and look back.* We are mirrored in the eyes of other people. If you want to know how you're perceived, you have to rely on other people to give you that information. But, if you want to evaluate yourself, you have to rely on imagination coupled with information. One way to "see ourselves as others see us" is to put ourselves in other people's shoes and take a look. Make a list of four people who know you well enough to be able to make judgments (favorable and unfavorable) about you. I suggest that you pick one friend (who loves you), one enemy (who doesn't love you), one supervisor (for whom you work), and one coworker (who works for you). Thinking about them one at a time, ask yourself how each would describe you in detail. Write as though you were speaking in their voices. At the top of a piece of paper, write the person's name and then "I think (your name) is ...." and then make a list of modifiers until you've reached the bottom of the page. For example, I would write: "Kate" (my wife, the friend).

Then I would write, "I think Mike is ... 1. handsome, 2. wonderful, 3. loving, etc." You get the picture. In speaking for Kate, I am trying to see myself, good and bad, through her eyes. (By the way, if I had continued my sample list for you, I eventually would have gotten to some bad, but not much ....)

When you're finished with all of your lists, put them together to form a sort of composite profile of yourself. You'll quickly discover that you're many things to many people. At first glance, you might appear to border on Multiple Personality Disorder. For example, my boss would never think I was as cute as Kate does (nor would I want that). The message you should get is that you are a multi-faceted, complicated creature who exhibits behaviors in some situations that are totally inappropriate in others where you mask them entirely. There are some ever-present character traits that you carry everywhere. Try not to favor one list over another. Avoid giving more credence to lists that focus on how wonderful you are. Frankly, you'll likely learn the most about yourself from evaluating your prickly relationships. Enemies and people who are hard on you reflect things you need to know about yourself.

3. *Compare yourself with other people.* Pick out one person you admire. List the qualities that make him or her impressive to you, then simply see how you stack up against him. This is an exercise in which you've engaged thousands of times in your life already. It started when you were a little kid who admired an adult and said, "I want to be just like that when I grow up!" However, as we grow up, two things become clear: that even our heroes have flaws, and that it's not possible to assume the identity of another person anyway. Nor would we want to. Undaunted, we merely narrow our focus. Instead of wanting to emulate someone cell by cell, we merely select specific traits or accomplishments. We try to press ourselves into those molds. The people around us provide us with a banquet feast of possibilities in human potential. We pick and choose. So, if you are trying to see yourself, a good way to do it is to compare and contrast yourself with someone who embodies skills, talents, and character traits you admire.

For example, let's assume that you admire your captain. He always stays on top of his paperwork. Everything is completed and turned in on time. Not only that, he also does everything neatly, and he keeps immaculate files. If you ask him for something, he knows right where it is. One of the qualities on your list of those you admire in him is "Good at managing paper." Now it's time for a quick reflection on yourself. Perhaps you're good at it, too. Or perhaps by comparison with the captain, you are woefully under his standard and have vast room for improvement. Or perhaps you fall somewhere in the middle. The point is that you have identified a skill you admire and have looked deeply into your own bag of tricks to see if it's there. If it isn't, you've got work to do.

4. Evaluate what happened the last time you felt proud and couldn't wait for your coworkers to see the stunning results of your efforts, and the last time you were so disappointed in yourself that you covered something up or denied your participation in it. One way to know how you're doing is to get brutally honest about how you feel when you complete an assignment or finish a job. At the extreme ends of the spectrum are feeling good and feeling bad. This is your personal version of "performance evaluation." When you do well or you're good at something, you stand by it. Even though it's occasionally important for other people to recognize your hand on the work and sing your praises, most of the time satisfaction is personal and private. Your success is applauded by a little standing ovation that only you can hear. You know you did well, and you know what you did to get it there. Good for you.

At the opposite end of the spectrum is knowing you've done badly. Like all of us, you've experienced those awful wrenching moments when you know you've screwed up. It's a double whammy. You're disappointed in yourself. But that's not the worst of it. You're also going to have to suffer the humiliation of admitting the error. It's natural to do everything you can to steel yourself against the firestorm of criticism that will rain down on your head the moment everyone else realizes that you've "really done it this time." One of the most effective ways to avoid criticism and consequence is to hide the mistake or at least deny your participation in it. It's the old "not my fault" routine. The worse the mistake, the more tempting the coverup. If you think back to the last time that you masked an error (or even thought about it), you'll discover a few important things about yourself. First, you are flawed. Big surprise! Second, the error and your reaction to it clearly define your value system. Third, you have to make specific changes in your life to make sure you don't repeat the error and to help you take responsibility next time. (There *will* be a next time, I assure you.)

I've given you examples of reactions to personal performance at opposite extremes. Most of the time, of course, you'll find yourself firmly entrenched somewhere in the middle. To evaluate how you're doing, get into the habit of examining your feelings about your work at every level. Small tasks. Monster projects. Teamwork. Pay particular attention to those things that you don't do well, for here's where you'll find the most room for improvement.

5. *Evaluate how other people react to you.* You've heard it said, "He must be a good guy because little kids and dogs seem to like him." This, of course, is a ridiculous generalization, but the point is that people (and obviously dogs) respond to hundreds of verbal and nonverbal cues you send out without even being aware that you're projecting an image. And they make pretty profound assumptions about you. In fact, when you first meet a person, he or she will formulate a complete profile on you within a few seconds. After you get to know each other, experience with you will shape and reshape those opinions—but not as much as you think. Hey, before you accuse the rest of the human race of being entirely too narrow-minded and far too quick to leap to conclusions, please know that you do the same thing. Still feeling indignant and self-righteous? Take this little test by completing the following sentences:

If she has "shifty" eyes, she can't be _____.

If he's fat, he must also be _____.

A man who wears a diamond stud earring is probably _____
_____.

A woman with the stethoscope is probably
   (1) a nurse or
   (2) a doctor.

A guy wearing the black leather jacket could be
  (1) a neurosurgeon or
  (2) a biker.

A person with a heavy Southern accent
  (1) might have a low IQ or
  (2) might be a Harvard grad.

When a man's handshake is clammy and limp, then you know that he's_____.

If she mispronounces your name as you're being introduced, then you know that she's _____.

If every hair on his head is sprayed into place, then you know he's _____.

If she's chewing gum, then you know she's _____.

Okay, now that the test is over, I'll tell you that it doesn't matter what you answered. If you had even a glimmer of an answer on just one of them, you're with the rest of us. We have all gathered information from our experience and culture to give us a set of standards—traits and behaviors that are consistent with personalities. Because we don't like to start from scratch with every introduction, we simply slap those standards against the new person and see how he or she measures up. Also, I'll tell you a horrible secret: We're lazy. It's much easier to make quick assumptions than it is to launch a fresh exploration with every new introduction. Hey, we have to start somewhere. The problem is that the lazier we are, the more apt we are to start and finish in the same second.

So what do you do with this lesson in human nature? Simply realize that these reactions and assumptions are being leveled at you every time you're in the company of another human being. If you can become attuned to reading the reactions and be willing to evaluate them, then you'll learn some things about the people around you. More important, however, is that you'll learn a lot about yourself: the image you project compared and contrasted with who you really are.

I'll give you an example. I used to work with a guy who was really gruff. He muttered everything in a low growl. New firefighters in the company were actually afraid of him. To be honest, so was I when I first came on board. But it didn't take me long to realize that he had a wry sense of humor and a deadpan delivery. If you listened, you were likely to catch wonderful one-liners and wicked sarcasm. He was hysterical. But the first impression that anyone had of him was that he was sinister. Of course, he didn't care. But if he had, he might have examined people's fearful reactions to him and adjusted his tone of voice or expression to match the hilarity just under the surface. When you get a reaction from someone, pay attention to it. It's mirroring the signals you just put out. If you get a reaction you didn't expect, then ask yourself, "What information did the person pick up? How was that perceived?" More important, "What can I do or say next time to send out more accurate signals?"

Let's take it one step further. We've been discussing isolated incidents and face-to-face encounters. There's much more. If you'll look at yourself in the context of the entire company, you'll discover that people around you have cast you into some sort of role—a position within the group. They're saying, "Oh, yeah, you can always count on him," or "You can never trust him to get things done right," or "He's the best driver we have," or "He's the worst cook in the bunch," or "We get nervous when we're on call with him," or "He's the guy you want by your side in a pinch." The list of judgments is endless. Everyone has one reserved just for you. If you want to know how you're doing, scan the organization and think about your relationship with each person. They're telling you what they think of you by their actions and their reactions to you. If you're astute, you can guess what their opinions are. If you want to formalize the process, take a sheet of paper and make two columns: "I'm best at ...." and "I'm worst at ...." Then list your coworkers. Go down the list, thinking as each person might. Decide what each one thinks are your best and worst skills or traits, and then make a little note about why you've made these decisions. For example, you might write, "John thinks I'm best at paperwork because he always asks me to proof his reports. John thinks I'm worst at starting an IV because he always hovers over me when we're on a medical call together, and I've noticed that he hesitates when I ask for the kit." So what can you learn from John's reactions? You're good at paperwork. He trusts your ability. He also trusts you enough as a friend to allow you to review his work, in spite of the chance that you will find errors. He thinks your skill in starting IVs isn't as great as his, but he regards your ability as adequate enough to override any urge he might have to take over. He respects you and is unwilling to do or say anything that would embarrass you. Personal performance evaluation conclusions? You need to continue to cultivate the trust of your coworkers. And you've got to get better at starting IVs. Good enough isn't good enough here. After you've evaluated yourself from John's point of view, move on through everyone in your organization.

By the way, trial lawyers master the principles of reaction and judgment to the point that they are able to manipulate perceptions artfully. They coach their clients and witnesses in clothing, hair styling, tone of voice, choice of words, facial expressions, body language, and manner to project appropriate images to juries. Attorneys know that, if you want the right reaction, you'd better be putting out the right signals. With practice, you might be able to do the same. Tackle a trait you want (but don't have) and "fake it 'til you make it." For example, if you want to be perceived as "willing to help" but frankly just don't have that kind of charity in you, it's possible to override your natural tendency to look the other way when a coworker is struggling with a task. Because you are engineering a perception, you can *act* "willing to help." You know what "willing to help" looks like. You merely put on the old smile and extend a good-natured offer to assist. If the person takes you up on it, continue to smile (in spite of your disappointment that now you're on the hook) and step in. When the task is done, you continue the act by graciously deflecting thanks with, "No problem. You would have done the same for me. It was my pleasure. Besides, you would have figured all of this out without me in another second." I said that you "fake it 'til you make it" because it doesn't take long for you to figure out that this (albeit faked) behavior is rewarding and not nearly as difficult as you thought. Before you know it, you are willing to help.

None of us are born with all of our skills and behaviors in place. No, we learn them as we go along. And it's never too late to learn.

How Good Are You at Evaluating Yourself?

Of course, seeing ourselves accurately is very difficult. One of three things happens whenever you turn that critical eye inward. If you think you're too wonderful for words, you'll find a way to turn negatives into positives. On the other hand, if you think you're not all you're cracked up to be, you'll run the new and improved you through a mental meat grinder. The third thing that could happen is that your vision will clear as you take a look, and you'll be able to see yourself as you really are. But a moment of clarity is rare, for we humans are experts at self-deception. In fact, true clarity is so infrequent that, when I experience it, I am at once suspicious of my own perceptions, as well I should be. All human beings have an uncanny knack for taking an unwelcome fact and twisting it into a more palatable work of fiction with a happy (or more acceptable) ending.

Let me give you an example of each scenario.

You suspect that you're not as good as you think you are. You're suddenly confronted with the disturbing realization that you can't keep up with your paperwork. If you could clearly see yourself in this situation, you might determine that you're disorganized and that you procrastinate because you find the task mind-numbingly dull. This would be the ugly truth. But admitting the truth would be inconsistent with your self-image that you're wonderful. Because you're a legend in your own mind, it's incomprehensible to you that you might be flawed and (slightly) weak in character. So you'll bypass the facts to justify your behavior by finding excuses. "I'm so busy doing really important things that I can't be bothered by mere paperwork. Besides, there's too much of it, anyway. Administration has gone overboard and out of their minds. No one gets it done. Hey, I get more of it done than probably anybody."

Truth: You're disorganized and you procrastinate.
Twist: You're a paragon struggling against an unrealistic task.

You suspect that you're better than you think you are. You're getting the impression that others think you're pretty good at teaching emergency evacuation procedures to your coworkers. Whoops!

After the workshop, they came up to you and said, "Thanks, buddy! You did a great job!" People whose self-esteem is intact will accept their accolades as well-deserved. Because you don't think you're very good at teaching, you dismiss their compliments as "pity praise." "They're just being nice. If they learned anything at all, it was in spite of me, not because of me. As soon as I turn my back, they'll confide in each other that I wasn't a very good teacher." There's no way on earth that you could be good at teaching. After all, you've had no training. You're just not very skilled at this sort of thing. If by chance you were good, it was dumb luck.

Truth: You're a good teacher.
Twist: You couldn't teach your way out of a paper bag.

You're right on the mark. In a practice drill, you poop out while hauling a hose. Instead of justifying your inability by accusing the drill supervisor of handing you a hose loaded with cement, you determine that you're not as well trained as you thought. You need to hit the gym. Or, in that same practice drill, you climb the tower faster than you've ever climbed it before. Instead of sneaking back later that night and secretly counting the steps to see if someone removed a few, you determine that your training has paid off. You've done well.

Truth: You know exactly what you're capable of achieving physically.
Twist: None!

There's an old adage: "To thine own self be true." In this case, I suggest that we rewrite it to read: "Of thine own self know true." Being clear about your strengths gives you the tools you need to function well and the confidence to use them. Knowing your weaknesses gives you the opportunity to compensate and improve and to become better at what you do and who you are.

360-Degree Feedback

You might be pretty good at evaluating yourself. And your supervisor might be pretty good at evaluating you. Between the two of you, you might get a pretty good handle on how you're doing. But there's a better way. A new method for evaluating employees is rapidly eclipsing the old standard performance evaluation. It's called 360-Degree Feedback because it allows an employee to have the benefit of multiple evaluations by people above, below, and parallel to him or her on the organization chart. This wider view of the person's performance is considerably more well-rounded and comprehensive than the observations of a single supervisor. Now used almost universally among *Fortune 500* companies, 360-Degree Feedback is proving to be effective.

The method is fairly simple. First, the company identifies a number of observable, measurable behaviors. Then the employee rates himself according to these behaviors. Then feedback is gathered from people with whom the employee interacts. Anonymously, they rate the employee on the same scale of behaviors. A human resources person attempts to identify consensus—group agreement on the ratings. Finally, the employee reviews the feedback.

The opinions of several people who are all in agreement will get the attention of an employee and force an honest appraisal of personal behaviors. Having the benefit of outside opinions is always a good idea because, frankly, we don't always see ourselves correctly. Research as far back as the 1920s confirms that we are inaccurate when we self-evaluate. Most of us tend to see things better than they are. Possibly, we know that our intentions are good, so we give ourselves extra points even if our results are under par. But research suggests that 360-Degree Feedback helps employees understand how the feedback is similar to or different from their own self-perceptions. Consequently, the feedback increases the accuracy of self-perceptions. Equally important, 360-Degree Feedback informs the employee that behaviors or skills are in need of improvement.

The people who are recruited to evaluate coworkers are trained before they begin the 360-Degree Feedback process. In addition, they are allowed to review anonymously, so they're protected from backlash if the person they're reviewing is displeased and prone to acts of recrimination.

Putting 360-Degree Feedback to Work for You

Unfortunately, not all organizations have 360-Degree Feedback in place. Even if your company doesn't have a formal system, you can still enjoy the benefits of 360-Degree Feedback on your own. Here are some simple tips for getting informal input from people all around you:

Decide that you really want to answer the question "How am I doing?" If you don't want the answer, don't ask the question.

Select a specific, measurable behavior or skill to evaluate. Avoid broad, sweeping, general traits like "being a good person" or "having fine values." It's nearly impossible to observe them, measure them, or remark on them.

Make a list of people in your organization who are in a position to observe you. Select folks from every level of the company.

Rate yourself. Be honest. Be brutally honest.

Take a deep breath and prepare to accept whatever feedback you get. One by one, take people aside and simply ask, "What do you think of my ability and performance in this specific area?" Be very careful how you word the question so that you don't influence the answer. David O. Selznick, famed Hollywood producer, used to solicit opinions of his films by saying, "Tell me how much you liked my movie!"

Make it clear that the reviewer is safe and sound. Nothing he says is going to have backlash. Listen without trying to defend or explain yourself.

If the feedback is gushing with praise (and this could happen because it's human nature not to want to hurt feelings), bend the interview around into a more productive direction by saying, "Why, thank you! But I'm looking for improvement. What do you think I could do to make it even better?"

Compare the responses of all of your reviewers and search for the consensus. Did they all agree? Did most agree? Are there a couple out in left field that need to be thrown out as invalid?

Compare the reviewers' remarks with your own evaluation.

What Does the Outcome of 360-Degree Feedback Mean to You?

Human resources experts have identified and interpreted several possible outcomes of 360-Degree Feedback. Notice that each one is balanced against consensus—the ability or inability to agree with the selected reviewers:

You overestimate your ability. Whoops! The feedback you got tells you that you aren't performing to the levels you thought. People who overestimate tend to make less effective decisions, have negative attitudes, think they don't need training or improvement, lack commitment to the job, and often conflict with other people at work. That's the bad news. The good news is that overestimators improve when they heed their feedback.

You underestimate your ability. The feedback tells you that you're doing better than you thought. People who underestimate tend to be moderately successful and effective, if humble, people. Unfortunately, like overestimators, they make ineffective decisions at work. They underachieve and consequently rarely realize their full professional potential. That's the bad news. The good news is that they're sort of easygoing and nonthreatening, so they're generally considered pleasant by coworkers. Also, they maintain pretty good performance levels and raise their self-perceptions when they pay attention to feedback.

You think you're doing well, and so do your reviewers. Consensus among your reviewers is a wonderful thing. And it gets even better when you agree, too. People who think they're good and get consensus from reviewers are successful and make effective decisions. They set high goals and achieve them. Their attitudes are great. Their commitment levels are high. Promotions come frequently. They rarely experience conflict with other people in the company. That's the good news. The even better news is that they are able to use any feedback constructively and realistically.

You don't think you're doing so hot, and neither do your reviewers. Okay, consensus might be wonderful, but not when you all agree that you're not performing up to par. People who think they're slacking and can confirm that with their reviewers are not successful performers. They make ineffective decisions. They have low skill levels, negative attitudes, low self-esteem, and low commitment to the job. That's the bad news. The worse news is that they'll often make no attempt to improve after feedback gives them a clear wake-up call.

What to Do With Feedback

You have two concerns: First, you have strengths and weaknesses to analyze, and second, you have the issue of consensus to consider. Both are equally important.

Strengths and weaknesses are the tools of your trade. If you've got strong skills and personal attributes, see if you can find ways to make them even stronger. If you've got deficiencies, figure out how to improve those ratings.

As for consensus, we learn from marketing experts that perception is often mistaken for reality. If you and your evaluators have a consensus, then you're all seeing the same things. You can be fairly certain that what you're seeing is valid and true. If you don't have a consensus, then something is out of whack. People don't perceive you as you really are, or you don't perceive yourself as you really are. Your mandate is to figure out what's wrong and get yourself in alignment with your evaluators, one way or the other. Then tackle your real strengths and real weaknesses.

Now That You've Got a Handle on Yourself, Apply the Principles to Other People

In the course of a leader's work, it is necessary to deliver feedback far more frequently than at an annual performance evaluation. People who work with you deserve to know what you're thinking. Not only does it help them feel more assured and secure, it also gives them clues about things they're doing right (so they can feel good) and things they're doing wrong (so they can improve performance). Unfortunately, praising and criticizing are tricky. Fortunately, I'm going to give you some pointers.

How to Praise Without Getting the Other Person All Sticky

I once worked for a captain who never remarked on my work. When our paths parted after many years together, he shook my hand and thanked me for the first time for a job well done. I couldn't resist the temptation to ask, "Sir, why in all these years didn't you tell me that I was doing a good job, and why didn't you ever thank me?" He replied, "When I hired you, I was looking for the best. I hired you. You were the best. You delivered the high performance I expected. I didn't know that I needed to point that out." Then he shrugged. End of discussion. Of course, he was right. But I often wonder how much more I might have accomplished had I been praised from time to time had I felt valued.

When you evaluate a person, it's important to include praise. But it's easy to get carried away with enthusiasm. Resist the urge. Praise too much, and you're seen as gushing and overly emotional. Your credibility goes right down the tubes. Praise too often, and you're seen as the village idiot who sees the bright side of everything, every day, all the time. Frankly, your words lose their meaning because they flow too freely. Also, your ability to judge is called into question. People will suspect you of sinister motives (you're obviously sucking up for some reason). Worst of all, when it comes time to criticize, you won't have a balanced platform from which to speak. Because you're seen as the cheerleader of all good things, when you have to address something unpleasant, your approach will be confusing. As important as praise is, it should be doled out judiciously, sparingly, and carefully.

In praising, try to stick to specific performances and avoid general personality assessments. Say, "You did great with that CPR!" Don't say, "You are a wonderful person!" As tempted as you might be, you aren't ever in position as a leader to take an isolated incident and expand it to reflect the entire person. In fact, great CPR can be performed by people who aren't wonderful and will never be made wonderful just because they can pump and blow. The person's character neither diminishes nor enhances the accomplishment. The accomplishment does not define the person's character. Don't confuse the two.

Human resources experts advise that you exercise extreme caution in praising employees. Praise is a double-edged sword. Without a doubt, enthusiastic praise has the power to inspire and motivate a person. On the other hand, it can backfire on you without warning. It can give an employee the mistaken impression that, because he is fabulous in one area, it isn't necessary to pay attention to other areas that might need improvement. After all, you said "Excellent!" and that was all the employee heard or needed to know. Consequently, you can find yourself working with a little swell-headed egomaniac who trades on one area of competence to the detriment of all else.

Another reason to tone it down is that the personnel file has to be realistic. There might be a lot right, but you need to document room for improvement. You're evaluating a human being, after all. No one is perfect. And things can go wrong. Every personnel director can tell you a horror story of an employee gone sour. This is human resources jargon for a person who, for some reason, suddenly ceases to be effective on the job ... and worse. The story always has an unhappy ending, especially when the supervisor comes down hard on the employee. Personnel files get opened, and glowing performance evaluations flutter to the attorney's floor. No one lives happily ever after. No one can reconcile the blinding gold stars and endless attaboys with this new, confusing contradiction. How can we possibly fire this paragon of virtue when it says in the official personnel file that perfection was exceeded at every juncture?

Constructive Criticism: Making the Bad Sound Good

Recently someone circulated a collection of witty remarks from British military personnel evaluations. My personal favorite was, "She continues to set low personal standards of performance and then fails to achieve them." It made me laugh, but it also brought to mind the difficulty in criticizing a person constructively. Frankly, it's not easy. When you tell someone that he is performing under acceptable standards, your observation is a personal assault. Feelings get hurt. Shields go up. Very few people can hear criticism without launching a defense. Human resources experts tell us that it can sometimes be helpful to preface a critical remark with an observation about something the person does really well. This lets the person know that you are credible. After all, you're smart enough to see how wonderful he is at this particular thing, and you're willing to tell the truth about it. Starting with a positive remark also gives the person a strong, dignified point on which to stand when, in a moment, you level some pretty harsh information at his fragile ego. And finally, the positive remark keeps the shields from going up immediately. The longer you can keep them down, the more the person will be able to hear. For example, you might need to tell a coworker that you found a glaring error in her report and that she needs to be more careful. You might say, "Dana, your reports are usually well done, but this one has a pretty serious mistake in it. We need to talk about what happened." This is much better than saying, "Dana, you blew this report."

Experts also warn us that criticism needs to be focused on the issue, not the person. In other words, you shouldn't say, "Dana, you're a moron." The minute the criticism gets personal, the discussion is really over. Stick to assessing tasks or behaviors, and leave the psychoanalysis out of it. You aren't qualified.

The final tip in delivering criticism and the part that makes it constructive is to seek resolution. Criticism without some plan for fixing the situation is useless. After you have stated the problem, give the person an opportunity to explain mitigating circumstances. Perhaps Dana blew the report because someone gave her wrong information. Maybe she wrote it at the end of a long shift and was really tired. Once you've heard the whole story, ask the person to suggest ways that would resolve the situation and prevent the problem in the future. And then be willing to help. If Dana erred because she had wrong information, she'll tell you that she really should have double-checked her source. You could offer to proof her reports before she turns them in. Or, you could suggest that she make notes on the reports that cite her sources. If she erred because she was tired, she'll tell you that she needs to do her reports earlier or to be more careful now that she knows that fatigue causes her to make mistakes. You could offer to adjust her schedule slightly. Or, you could suggest that she put a sticky-back warning label on reports that are written when she's tired so that you'll be alerted to the need to proof them. No matter what the problem, you need to work out the resolution together. The resolution has to be specific and measurable so you'll both know that things are, in fact, improving. If the person says, "I'll do better," ask, "Step by step, how?" and "When specifically will we see the improvement?"

Judge Lest Ye Be Judged

We, as people, are constantly judging each other. We can't help it. In everyday life, judging can be as simple as noticing a personality trait and then comparing and contrasting it with something similar in your own set of traits. However, judging—evaluating—becomes a vital skill when you're a leader. You not only have to see people, their abilities, and their performances with perfect clarity, you also have to be able to bring them into alignment with the high standards you set for your department. Never forget that you are one of the people who must remain under your watchful eye.

PERSONAL STUDY EXERCISES

1. Find a person who is struggling on a job, and praise one aspect of his effort. Make it short, sweet, and casual. Notice whether or not your praise gives that person a little boost of confidence and enhances his performance.

2. Think about the last time you were misunderstood or something you said was misinterpreted. Specifically, how did you cause that?

3. Find people in your organization you respect and ask them, "How am I doing?" Compare their responses with your own opinions. Notice how they are different.

Epilogue

Remember that leadership isn't a moment of arrival. It's a life-long process. You can't study a few books, attend a few seminars, pass an exam, and then graduate as a "Leader." There's no certificate. No diploma. No special ribbon on your uniform. And yet, it's the most important credential you'll carry in your career—far more influential and valuable than rank. It separates you from the mediocre and mundane, and elevates you to the highest ideals that human beings can embrace. It's the force and power within you that you'll use to accomplish great things and do great work. Leadership allows you to partner with other people to reach for things that are without question beyond a mere mortal's grasp, and to achieve success beyond your wildest imagination. Under your leadership and together, you and the people around you will equal far more than the sum of your parts.

As a leader, you'll have to re-earn the respect of people every day. Every minute is a new test. Every situation is a previously unanswered question. Every decision is a brand-new answer. You'll never rest.

After searching for the definition of "leader" so you'll know what to do to be one, you've discovered that a concrete definition is frustratingly elusive. Although few have even come close to identifying all of the qualities and attributes that define a leader, you know that you've never had to rely on the observations of scholars to know a leader when you see one. For as long as you've been alive, you've instinctively known. We humans don't quite know what it is, but we know leadership when we see it.

And you know that we all possess leadership. Some of us are just better at stepping forward and lighting the way for other people. Right now you're doing everything you can to make the leap. Through study, thought, and personal action, you're honing those skills that you've identified as valuable. I congratulate you and I know you'll succeed.

Just when you think that you've got it all figured out, I have to remind you of one thing more. You, like every great leader, have a responsibility to nurture and develop talented people—other leaders—in your organization. You have to be generous enough to build a safe culture for their personal and professional development so that they'll have the benefit of opportunities to grow. Additionally, be accessible so that they can know you and observe you up close. Your life can teach them a lot. Not only will they follow you, they'll also follow your example. You could be the genesis for a whole new generation of great leaders who will practice their art by your example. Success begets success. Remember that the best leader is one who remembers how he or she followed.

The process of reaching back and taking other people with you into leadership begins before the ink is dry on your new contract, and it ends when you retire and leave your organization in their capable hands. The results of an entire organization of leaders in development? Smooth sailing, satisfied employees, unencumbered teamwork, and a culture of creative men and women committed to a common effort without fear or hesitation.

I wish you every success!